INVE$TOR'S
—PLAYBOOK—
GET OFF THE SIDELINES

A SIX STEP PROCESS TO FINANCIAL FREEDOM

VOL. 2

DESHAWN EDWARDS

CORNELL ROWAN

Published by Investor's Playbook LLC

ACKNOWLEDGMENT

To those who poured into us, not through loud speeches or formal lectures, but through quiet lessons, real-life examples, and conversations that planted seeds long before we understood their value.

Your subtle nudges sparked something greater than you could have imagined. A mindset shift. A moment of clarity. A new direction. The knowledge you shared, intentionally or unknowingly, changed how we saw money, opportunity, and the power of ownership.

Because of your influence, we learned that money is not just something to earn or save. It is a tool to be directed, a resource to be multiplied, and a pathway to build something lasting. You showed us that financial literacy is more than numbers... it is power, responsibility, and legacy.

This playbook was born from the seeds you planted. Your example became the foundation for everything we've built, and now it is our mission to extend that same knowledge and inspiration to others. We hope these pages reflect the impact you had on us.

With heartfelt gratitude, we thank you.

TABLE OF CONTENTS

INTRODUCTION
The Rules Haven't Changed, You Just Had the Wrong Playbook

There was a time when financial success followed a simple formula: go to school, get a good job, save money, avoid bad debt, and retire comfortably. That was the advice passed down from parents, teachers, mentors, and it made sense for a different era.

Back then, a single income could support a household, rent took up a reasonable portion of your paycheck, gas was cheap, and checking out at the grocery store made sense. A time when college was affordable, and jobs were stable enough to allow people to work and retire with a pension, living out the rest of their lives in relative peace. But that time is gone.

Today, we live in a world where prices increase faster than promotions, rent costs an arm and a leg, and a degree can cost six figures, and still leave you underemployed. While wages have increased, the cost of everything that matters has increased even more. Healthcare, housing, childcare, food, even peace of mind comes at a premium now.

The game changed, but no one handed us the right playbook...

Instead, most people are still trying to win using outdated strategies. They're working long hours, trying to save what they can... and yet somehow, it still feels like they're stuck in quicksand. Moving, grinding, doing everything right, but getting nowhere fast.

We see it in every generation. If you're a Millennial, you might be trying to buy your first home while paying back student loan debt and raising your new family. Gen Z's have entered adulthood in a post-pandemic world filled with automation, gig work, and financial uncertainty. Even Gen X and Boomers are feeling the squeeze, realizing retirement might not be what they imagined.

Information moves faster than ever. And those who understand how to use money, systems, and strategy are quietly pulling ahead while everyone else plays catch-up, confused about why hard work alone isn't enough anymore.

Let's be clear: this isn't about fear... it's about awareness.

It's not that financial freedom is impossible. It's that we've been thoroughly misinformed.

It's not just about how much you earn, it's about how well you use what you keep. It's about multiplying, protecting, and letting your money grow while you sleep.

There's a familiar story that plays out all the time... maybe you've lived it. You get a raise, and you're excited for a few months. But somehow your bills stretch to match your new pay, and your expenses rise without your permission. You swear to yourself that you're doing better, but the new money starts to not feel any different.

This isn't bad math, that's the system working as it is designed, keeping you spending, stuck, and searching for a way out.

You're not alone, and you aren't broken, you are simply following a playbook that has never led anyone to success. The good news is you can catch up, or even better, get ahead, if you're willing to shift how you think. This book is your permission to stop following dead-end advice and start building a life that will actually grant you the life you're longing for. Because here is the truth... nobody is coming to save you. Not the government, not your employer, and most likely not the lottery.

The people who are winning today are the ones who treat money like a skill, something you study, practice, and master. They build systems and learn how to invest. They understand the tax code, use credit as a tool, and value freedom over being flashy. Wealth isn't about working tirelessly, it's about working smart. That is what this playbook is all about.

You don't have to follow the old way of thinking, in fact, we are going to show you how to change that mindset with intention and purpose. Change starts with being aware. So may this book bring awareness and an everlasting change to you and your loved ones.

Why Saving Isn't Enough

Most of us grew up hearing one piece of financial advice on repeat: "Save your money."

It came from people who loved us; parents, grandparents, or mentors. They saw saving as the safest, smartest way to stay afloat. Many were never introduced to investing so to them saving was the best course of action.

But saving isn't enough... Inflation eats away at your money every year. While you're trying to be responsible, the cost of living keeps rising, and your hard-earned savings quietly lose power. What felt like security a decade ago now feels like standing still in a race where the finish line keeps moving.

Between bills, paying down debt, and life pulling you in every direction, it's easy to feel like you're saving just to spend it on the next emergency, unexpected charge, or the next setback. We aren't saying that saving is bad, but it should be the beginning of your journey towards financial freedom.

Saving can build discipline, it can give you breathing room, but it doesn't always translate to wealth, and it rarely creates freedom. To buy back your time and build something bigger, you need a plan to put your money to work. Saving is where you start, ownership is where you grow, and strategy is how you scale. The goal of this playbook is to move you from survival to momentum, and from there, to real wealth.

How to Use This Playbook

This isn't just something you read and shelf, it's a playbook to study, run, and return to when the game gets tough or the next level is calling.

We wrote this for people with goals. People who dream of being free from high-interest debt but fear that it is impossible. People who are tired of sitting on the sidelines, watching others build wealth while they wait for the "right time"

So let's make this clear from the jump:

Using this playbook is simple, but only if you're ready to get off the sidelines.

You don't need to have all the answers or be perfect. You just need to move!

Each play in this book walks you through a core pillar of financial success. Inside every play are short, focused chapters. Some are practical, some are mindset-shifting, and some might make you uncomfortable. Take the discomfort as a good sign. It just means growth is happening.

You can go in order, or you can jump to where you need the most help, just don't stay still. Pick a chapter, read it with intention, and then act. The key here is that you start. Every play in this book is actionable. When it calls for a step to be made, take it. When it drops a challenge, accept it! And when it hits you with a truth, sit with it.

Bookmark the chapters that hit you the hardest and reread the ones that ask more of you. Bring it with you into conversations, financial planning sessions, or decision-making moments. This playbook isn't a book you finish, it's a resource you can always come back to.

If you're ready to stop watching from the sidelines and start building, this is your playbook. Let's get to work!

FIRST PLAY

LAY THE FOUNDATION OF FINANCIAL SUCCESS

CHAPTER 1

Money Mindset: What Do You Really Believe About Money?

Before you earn your next dollar, before you save another cent, before you invest in any stock, real estate, or business, you have to answer one question:

What do you really believe about money?

Not what you tell yourself you believe, but what you *really* believe. Because your mindset is your financial operating system. And like any system, if it's outdated or full of bugs, nothing else will run the way it's supposed to, regardless of how much money you make.

Let's get real. If you grew up like most of us then your money mindset wasn't built by financial planners or wealth coaches. It was built in everyday moments like watching your parents stress about bills, hearing phrases like "money doesn't grow on trees," or being taught to never talk about money at all.

Maybe you saw money as stressful or scarce. You might have been told that rich people are greedy or that talking about money is boasting. Maybe deep down you feel like financial freedom isn't for you.

That's mindset, and it's running your financial life whether you realize it or not.

The truth is, most people stay stuck financially because their belief system never changed, even when their income did.

They make more money but still live check to check. They save a little but feel guilty spending. They avoid investing because it feels like gambling. Or they make one mistake and spiral into shame.

You can't out-earn a broken mindset.

Having a wealthy mindset means thinking differently and moving differently. It's seeing money as a tool, not a reward. The wealthy believe in ownership over image and they focus on long-term value, not instant gratification. They're willing to learn, take calculated risks, and course-correct along the way.

The difference between a scarcity mindset and a wealthy mindset is not magic, it's mentality.

The best part about this is that you can choose to change your mindset today, right now. But it starts with awareness.

Start by asking yourself these questions:

- Do I see money as something I can control or something that controls me?
- Do I believe there's *enough* to go around?
- When I hear the word "wealth," what emotions show up? (fear, envy, confidence, curiosity?)
- Do I believe I'm capable of being wealthy, or do I feel like I missed my shot?

Questions like these are the the foundation of every financial decision you make. Your mindset determines how you spend, save, invest, and respond to setbacks.

If you want to build a new financial future, you have to build a new belief system.

Below are some examples of ways you can shift from having a scarcity mindset to a strategic/wealthy mindset:

Scarcity says: "I'll never get ahead."
Strategy says: "What's my next best move?"

Scarcity says: "There's not enough to go around."
Strategy says: "There's always opportunity if I learn how to see it."

Scarcity says: "I'm bad with money."
Strategy says: "I can learn to get better with money."

Every time you shift from emotional reaction to intentional response, your mindset levels up, and so does your life.

We are not asking you to act like the intricacies of money aren't hard, we are asking you to stop believing that you are not capable of mastering it. This chapter calls on you to see your responsibility. Once you understand that your thoughts shape your reality, the next step is to accept that you are ultimately responsible for what you choose to think next.

That understanding is what makes this the first and most important play in the entire book. Everything that follows is built on the foundation of how you view wealth. Not just what you do with your money, but how you carry yourself and who you are becoming along the way.

So... ask yourself again:

What do I really believe about money?

Be honest with your answer, write it down, reflect on it, challenge and change what no longer serves you. Then make the choice to shift your mindset and move forward with clarity and confidence!

Before going to the next chapter, let's do a money mindset self-check audit.

Using any word at your disposal, complete the sentences below to get a gauge on how you feel about money and finances.

You can use multiple words for one answer. At the end of the First Play, you'll revisit your responses to see what has potentially shifted.

Complete the sentences by filling in the blank:

1. Right now, money feels ______
2. Growing up, money seemed ______
3. When I think about wealthy people, they seem ______
4. My current relationship with money is ______
5. Trying to build wealth feels ______
6. Managing my finances has been ______
7. If I'm being honest, my money mindset today is ______

CHAPTER 2

Cash Flow Clarity:
Track It, Own It, Optimize It

If money is a tool, then your wealth plan is the blueprint that tells you where your tools are, how your tools are being used, and where your tools might be getting lost. It doesn't matter how much you make if you don't know where it's going.

This is where most people start to go wrong... They assume that earning more money will solve everything. In most cases, making more money won't hurt, but if you have bad money habits, more money only amplifies the current negative behavior. If you don't have a system to handle you making $2,000 a month, you'll have chaos when you're making $10,000. That is why cash flow clarity is foundational.

Track It

Let's start with the basics: you need to know every dollar that comes in, and every dollar that goes out. Not just a rough estimate, not in your head, and not saying "I think I'm doing okay." You need to see it in black and white.

This doesn't mean you need to become a spreadsheet junkie or obsess over every $5 latte, but if you don't know your numbers, you're guessing. And guessing is not a wealth-building strategy.

A great place to start is by tracking your income, and not just your paycheck, but every single source of money. Every side hustle, refund check, tip, or bonus.

Now here is the hard part... write down all of your expenses. Go look back at your credit card statement one full month prior and write down everything.

Start with the easy items like your fixed expenses. These items are, for the most part, are unchangeable from month to month. (rent/mortgage, insurance, credit card payments, car note, cell phone bill, and even your Netflix subscription). Everything that has a relatively fixed price should go on this list.

Next, you want to write down your variable expenses. This is anything that is a regular monthly expense, but the amount can vary and depends on what you do that month (groceries, gas, household supplies, dining out, entertainment, personal care, etc.)

Lastly, you have your utilities. They're in their own category. They are monthly and essential, but the cost can fluctuate. Let's add them to the essential semi-fixed expenses category.

Now, we just asked you to do a lot, but take your time and make sure you don't miss anything. The most important reminder is to not judge yourself based on the results. This exercise is simply for you to see where your money is going, because what you can't see, you can't control.

Own It

Once you see where your money is going, it's time to take ownership. If your cash is disappearing on impulse buys or unplanned spending, that's not a failure, that's information! Use it, learn from it, and adjust where needed.

Ownership means refusing to play the blame game. It's not your job's fault, and it's not inflation's fault. Don't blame your parents, or your kids, or even your ex. Ownership is taking responsibility and realizing that the one in control is you. There are outside factors happening in your life, most definitely, but how you choose to respond is ultimately up to you.

Cash flow clarity means being honest and intentional about your spending. Every dollar you earn has a job. It can build your future, or it can fund your distractions. You choose.

This is where discipline meets design. You can start to see patterns, and you should start to notice what actually matters and what's just noise. Once you own your patterns, you can start to take control and make better financial habits. Don't just drift in the lazy river of life, after you track your spending, and own your habits, you are ready to go to the next step of clarity... optimization!

Optimize It

Now that you know what's happening and you've taken ownership, let's get to optimizing. This is where you start to make better choices. This is more than just increasing the amount you save. Optimizing means spending more wisely and creating margin. Margin is defined as the gap between what you make and what you spend. Wealth is built by increasing your margin.

The fastest way to increase margin is to make changes in the way you spend. Making more money helps too, but that isn't always an immediately choice. Here are a few smart ways to optimize your cash flow and increase your margin:

- Cut or cancel what no longer serves you (subscriptions, low-impact purchases, late fees).
- Set spending limits on categories that tend to run wild.
- Use cash-back tools, automation, or bank accounts that reward good habits (more on these later).
- Use extra cash to pay down high-interest debt, invest, or build an emergency fund. Avoid lifestyle upgrades for now.

The goal isn't to be cheap, it's about being strategic. Optimization is taking the same income and getting more out of it. After you master optimization, you are now in control of your cash flow.

There's true power in knowing exactly what is happening with your money. You walk with more confidence, you are able to make faster decisions, and when bills hit, you aren't surprised. But the best feeling is the ability to act when an opportunity presents itself. Imagine feeling in control simply because you are aware. Not because you are rich, but because you have clarity. Cash flow clarity gives you options, and in this book we explain that options are freedom. So, before we even start talking about tackling debt, investing, or building passive income, you first need to master the art of cash flow clarity. Track it, own it, optimize it. Remove the “guess” out of guesswork, and lets get to work!

CHAPTER 3

Emergency Fund = Confidence Fund

Most people think an emergency fund is just a financial cushion, or a pile of cash sitting there "just in case."

But it's much more than that.

An emergency fund is a confidence fund that allows you to move through life without constantly looking over your shoulder. It gives you options (freedom), and it gives you breathing room.

Now I will be honest... everyone might not feel like they need an emergency fund, and that is ok. But when you are one unexpected bill away from chaos, an emergency fund can provide you with a necessary dose of relief. Your emergency fund is your defense. It's what keeps the basics covered when life hits you out of nowhere, and life seems to always hit when we least expect it.

So what's the target?

You can always start with a buffer, building an emergency fund of $1,000, and eventually working your way towards three to six months of essential expenses. And when we say essential, we mean **ESSENTIAL!** This doesn't need to fund your full lifestyle, just what it takes for you to stay afloat: rent, utilities, food, transportation, insurance, the must-haves. And to make the deal even better, and make sure you place this money in a High-Yield Savings Account (HYSA). This type of savings account can grow your emergency fund at a much faster rate than a traditional savings account. Look for an account that will give you at least a 3.5% Annual Percentage Yield (APY) return on your money. This way you are not just stuffing money into a mattress. It's actually growing!

As you start this process, remember that this isn't about perfection, it's all about progress. This is something you build dollar by dollar, and choice by choice.

Once the money is in the HYSA, treat it like it isn't there.

Don't touch it for vacations.
Don't "dip into it" because a new sale hit your inbox.
Don't count it as "extra money" on a good month.

You protect this fund because it protects you.

The moment you have money set aside, your energy shifts. You start making decisions from security, not stress. You breathe differently and you think bigger. You stop reacting and start responding.

That's why this is more than a financial step to success; it's a psychological step. So call it what it really is, your confidence fund.

And you need it if you're serious about wealth.

CHAPTER 4

Wealth Planning > Budgeting

If you've ever frowned at the word budget, you're not alone.

Most people hear "budget" and think of restriction, sacrifice, or boredom. Basically a spreadsheet that tells you what not to do. And while budgeting has its place, especially right after tracking your expenses, it's not the whole game.

However, we're going to rebrand this term in our mind. It's about planning for wealth with purpose, freedom, and vision. We are not just "budgeting". We are "wealth planning!"

Wealth planning is forward facing and says: "Here's where I want my money to go and grow," and helps you align with your values and goals, while minimizing unnecessary expenses.

Wealth planning comes after you've done the hard work of tracking your patterns and taking ownership. Now that you know where your money's been, it's time to decide where it's headed next.

The Wealth Planning Framework

Instead of limiting your spending, start directing your dollars. By giving every dollar a destination, you are basing your wealth plan on your vision, and not on your bills.

Here's the breakdown:

1. Mandatory / Fixed Expenses
These are the non-negotiable items and the things you must pay to stay afloat and functioning:
- Rent or mortgage
- Utilities
- Phone
- Transportation
- Insurance
- Debt minimums

We aren't optimizing here, we're acknowledging what's essential to live and operate.

2. Variable Expenses
These are the flexible monthly costs that still matter:
- Groceries
- Gas
- Dining out
- Shopping
- Kids' activities
- Streaming services

You don't need to eliminate these either, just be aware of the rhythm.

3. Savings + Emergency Fund Contributions
Every month should include something going to future you, even if it's $25.

4. Investments
This is where the wealth gets built! Brokerage accounts, IRAs, retirement funds, digital assets (crypto), real estate, or whatever lane you're working in. Don't wait until "what's left over" to invest. Make it part of the plan now, even if it's small.

And finally the last step in your wealth plan...

5. Free Spending / Joy Fund
Yes, include this intentionally.
Spend your remaining money on things you want. Feel like going to catch a movie? That's what these funds are for. Or maybe putting more towards your debt would make you happy, accelerate your financial freedom journey. Regardless of what you deicide, planning for enjoyment removes the guilt of spending and keeps you moving towards your goals without back pedaling.

This is where your money starts reflecting your values. It gives you a monthly playbook to adjust, refine, and stick to, even when life changes. And the best part? Once you've planned your wealth, budgeting becomes automatic. Clear intentions, and clear decisions.

We will end The First Play with a phrase of affirmation:

You Are the CFO of Your Life

Wealth doesn't get built by accident, it comes from making a decision. Don't wait on the perfect plan to find your starting point. Restriction is not the goal, instead think intention. This is the first step to go from surviving your paycheck to strategically building your future.

Budgeting is maintenance.
Wealth planning is momentum.

You already tracked where your money went. Now decide where it's going next.

Now that your plan is in motion, it's time to free yourself from the weight holding it back.

Let's tackle the debt that's draining your momentum and flip the script from owing money to owning your future.

SECOND PLAY

PAY DOWN HIGH-INTEREST DEBT

CHAPTER 5

The Real Cost Of Debt (It's More Than Money)

Let's get one thing straight:

Debt is not just a number, it's a weight. And most people have been carrying it so long, they forget what it feels like to move freely. We've been told debt is normal, a necessary step to progression. And though that might be true for good debt (less than 10% interest), bad debt is a different story.

We swipe for our wants, take out loans for things we can't afford, and all this to impress people who won't remember us the next day. It's so common it doesn't even feel like a crisis anymore.

But the harsh reality is that high-interest debt is one of the most effective traps ever created to keep people from building real wealth. Worst of all, it doesn't just drain your wallet. It saps your energy, focus, confidence, and your options (freedom).

Let's say you owe $8,000 on a credit card with a 22% interest rate. You pay the minimum each month, not because you want to, but because that's all you can manage right now. At that rate, it will take you about 20 years to pay it off... and you'll spend more than double what you originally borrowed. That $8,000 will cost you nearly $17,000!

Now multiply that across multiple cards, add in buy-now-pay-later plans, personal loans, payday loans, and the list goes on and on. You're not just paying interest, you're paying for time you've already lived. You're paying more tomorrow for decisions you made yesterday. And you already know the lenders love it! They profit off of your delay, your fatigue, and your silence.

Debt doesn't just hit your balance sheet, it attacks your mindset. It can make you feel behind before you even start, and robs you of momentum.

Ask yourself, have you ever said something like this:

"I can't save right now, because I'm already in the hole."

or

"I don't have money to invest, because I need to pay off my credit cards first"

You turn down and miss out on potential growth opportunities, because your credit score is wrecked or your cash is tied up in payments.

And so you stall...

Bad debt turns ambitious, creative, resourceful people into hesitant, exhausted, reactive ones. This isn't because you're weak, it's because the weight of debt is real.

Many people reading this make enough money to build wealth, but they can't get ahead because their cash is already spoken for. Every paycheck is sliced up before it even hits the account. Interest, minimums, fees, due dates, it's like running a race where someone keeps moving the finish line.

It's not that you're not working hard enough, it's that the system is set up to make you serve your past instead of investing in your future. But here's what they don't expect:

They don't expect you to wake up, get clear, and take back control.

Debt Should Have A Purpose

We mentioned this earlier, but not all debt is evil. Smart debt can open doors and create opportunities in business, education, investing, and provide leverage when needed. We will dive deeper into this in a later play.

However, high-interest consumer debt? That is not strategic, it's shackles in disguise. It's built to extract instead of empower. And if you're chained to negative compound interest, it will be extremely difficult to build peace and stability.

Luckily you can change your trajectory.

This play is all about creating a real plan to pay off high-interest debt and stop feeding the debt machine.

This play is about reclaiming every dollar, every ounce of energy, and every option that debt has stolen from you. I can't promise that it will be a fast and easy victory, but it will definitely be worth it. Because the real cost of debt isn't just money, it's how it puts your dreams on hold... and you've waited long enough.

We created a debt calculator to assist you as you walk through the next chapter. This resource is not required, but can serve as a handy tool to document your debt payment strategy. Scan the QR code and find the Investor's Playbook Debt Strategy Calculator Link. Follow the instructions and if needed, export a local copy.

Investor's Playbook

LinkTree → Debt Strategy Calculator

CHAPTER 6

Avalanche vs. Snowball: Pick Your Weapon

By now, you know debt is costing you more than you thought. Now it's time to fight back. But here's the secret to winning this war: you don't fight debt with hope. You fight debt with a plan. A plan that works with your brain, your cash flow, and your real life.

There are two proven strategies to knock out debt:

- The Avalanche Method
- The Snowball Method

They're both powerful and which one you choose depends on your personality, your priorities, and your motivation style.

Let's break them down.

The Avalanche Method - The Logical Technique

The Avalanche Method targets your highest-interest debt first.

You make minimum payments on all your debts, then throw any extra money at the account with the highest Annual Percentage Rate (APR).

Once that one is gone, you roll all of that freed-up money into the next highest-interest debt, and so on.

This method saves you the most money in the long run, because you're killing off the most expensive debt first.

Check out the example below:

Let's say you've got:

- $5,000 credit card #1 at 24% APR, $150 minimum
- $4,000 personal loan at 14% APR, $100 minimum
- $2,000 credit card #2 at 19% APR, $50 minimum

You've got an extra $300/month to throw at debt. Under the Avalanche Method, you'd pay:

- $150 minimum to first card + $300 extra = $450 total/month
- $100 minimum to the loan
- $50 to the second credit card

Once that 24% monster is gone, all of that money ($450) gets rolled into the next-highest APR (the 19% store card), and so on. Like the method suggests, you're stacking your payments like an avalanche, crushing interest and saving hundreds, or even thousands over time. Now let's take a look at the "feel good" approach to tackling debt.

The Snowball Method - The Psychological Win

The Snowball Method is all about momentum and has you target your smallest balance first, regardless of the interest rate. You pay the minimum on everything, but throw extra money at the smallest debt until it's gone. Then you roll that money into the next smallest balance, and repeat. This method gives you quick wins that build motivation. This works perfectly if you need to feel progress fast and helps you stay emotionally engaged. Here is another example, but this time we use the snowball method.

Using the same debts:

- $5,000 credit card #1 at 24%
- $4,000 loan at 14%
- $2,000 credit card #2 at 19%

You'd throw all your extra firepower at the $2,000 credit card first. The goal is the same, but you would pay more by the end, due to having balances on the cards with higher interest for a longer amount of time. The trade-off is the psychological win and the feeling you get from completely wiping out one debt. It gives you the fuel to keep going that builds to consistency. And consistency pays off more than perfection ever could.

So, which weapon should you choose?

- If you're motivated by logic and long-term savings, go **Avalanche**.
- If you're driven by momentum and fast wins, go **Snowball.**

Both work. But you have to commit.

Don't spend the next three months "thinking about it." Pick one, write it down, name your enemy, and build your attack plan. Make a move.

The moment you pay off one debt, you don't stop. You roll that same payment into the next one. That's where the magic happens. It's called debt stacking, and it works because you keep the pressure on. You free up money and redeploy, eventually turning that momentum into freedom.

You don't need a perfect credit score to start, and you don't need a raise. You need a plan, a little discipline, and a reason that's bigger than your excuses. Every dollar you send toward debt is a payment towards your future. You don't have to carry this forever, and you can start where you are right now. Use what you have, and don't stop stacking until it's gone.

Debt is loud, but freedom is louder.

CHAPTER 7

Side Hustles & Power Payments

You're making moves now! Feels good right? You've chosen your weapon and you've mapped out your debt. But the part people miss about paying off debt is direction.

Too many people start attacking their balances like a warrior, and then, three weeks later, they're using the same credit card again, just to buy groceries. They made a big move without a smart plan, and the debt cycle starts all over again. Let's fix that.

Being Aggressive is Good, Being Reckless Is Not

There's nothing wrong with wanting to throw large payments at your debt. In fact, that's how you win. But don't pay down debt so aggressively that you end up needing more debt to survive. You shouldn't be sending $1,000 to a credit card if that means you'll be over-drafting next week, or swiping it again for gas. That's going in circles, rather than moving toward financial freedom. Instead, you need a two-part strategy:

1. Use your main income to cover your minimum payments.
2. Use extra income to make *power payments.*

This keeps your cash flowing and your bills covered.

Let's actually define what a power payment is, and what it looks like. Any money above the minimum that you apply toward a targeted debt is considered a power payment. This is the extra firepower that actually moves the needle and shortens timelines. It also drastically cuts interest and builds momentum. Where does this extra cash come from though? This is where we move to the topic of side hustles.

You don't need to start a business overnight. The key here is to find a way to make extra cash and funnel that money into your freedom plan. Listed below are a few tried-and-true side income ideas:

- Freelance a skill (graphic design, writing, social media, video editing)
- Sell unused items online (Facebook Marketplace, OfferUp, LetGo)
- Deliver or drive (Uber, DoorDash, Instacart)
- Tutoring or coaching (test prep, fitness, language, life skills)
- Turn a hobby into income (candles, crafts, digital art, printables)
- Seasonal work (event gigs, tax prep, catering, retail peak seasons)

These aren't meant to be forever gigs, but temporary surges in cash that fuel your debt payoff strategy.

Just to bring it home, let's run through an example of how a side gig can accelerate you snowball/avalanche method.

Let's say you pick up a weekend gig delivering for Instacart. You work 6 hours on Saturday, and make $120.

That's $480 a month without touching your main job.

Now apply that as a *power payment* to your highest-interest credit card, on top of your minimum. (Using the Avalanche Method)

- You were paying $150 a month → now you're paying $630
- What would've taken 3 years now takes less than one
- And you've saved hundreds, or even thousands in interest

Of course this is just an example and depending on location, your available "free time," and the time you decided to read this book, your numbers could look quite different. Ultimately, this isn't magic, it's math. And the formula is: **money + momentum + a plan = freedom.**

Let's review what we learned in this chapter and how to stack your wins without backtracking:

■ Have your minimum expenses covered
■ Keep your emergency fund intact (or at least growing)
■ Keep track of your cash flow
■ Apply side hustle income directly to debt, not your lifestyle

You don't want to make huge payments just to feel broke the rest of the month.

You don't want to swipe a card after you just paid it down.

And you definitely don't want to sacrifice stability just to feel productive.

Freedom from high interest debt is the goal, but realistic and sustainable progress is how you get there. Try this exercise next time you send in a power payment.

With each power payment, visualize what you're buying back with that money.

- $Less stress
- $More control
- $A stronger credit profile
- $A future without chains
- $Options (Freedom)

Don't let debt define you, instead let your decisions determine how long debt remains part of your story.

In the next chapter we will talk about the other half of the debt journey: How to stay out of debt. And trust us, once you taste this kind of freedom, you'll never want to go back.

CHAPTER 8

Temptation Killers: Stay Out Once You're Out

We know that paying off debt takes effort, but staying out of debt? That my friend, takes discipline, self-awareness, and better systems. Temptation doesn't disappear just because your balance hits zero.

The algorithm is still pushing flashy sales.
Friends are still flexing their latest upgrades.
Your emotions still want to be soothed when life gets stressful.

And your credit card company? They're patiently waiting for you to slip up again. The system is literally designed to pull you back into debt and stress. So you've got to build a system of your own. One that blocks temptation before it wreaks havoc on all your progress.

Let's bring something to the light really quickly... debt is emotional.

People don't usually go into debt because they are unintelligent or lazy. They go into debt because they are trying to solve a problem, and they want the solution to come quickly and quietly.

If you're bored, you shop.
If you're stressed, you take a vacation.

Long day at work? You order from a delivery service. Felling behind in life? You buy a "flex item" to feel better.

The purchase gives you exactly what you are looking for, which is a short-term relief. But not long after, the credit card statement hits... Then comes the guilt, the worry, and before you know it, the cycle starts all over again.

This chapter is about breaking that loop without relying on willpower, but instead with systems and self-awareness.

Story Time!

Meet Brodie: Brodie paid off $6,500 in credit card debt over 14 months. He was focused, locked in, and proud of the progress.

But then came his cousin's wedding. He didn't want to show up in old clothes, so he put a new suit on his card.

A month later, his car needed tires. He didn't want to drain his emergency fund, so he charged it.

Then his friends planned a last-minute getaway. "I deserve it," he told himself. Swipe!

By the end of the year, Brodie was back up to $4,200 in credit card debt. This didn't happen because he wasn't smart; it happened because he never built a system to resist the temptation. For you, that stops here.

Long day at work? You order from a delivery service. Felling behind in life? You buy a flex item to feel better.

The purchase gives you exactly what you are looking for, a short-term relief. But not long after, the credit card statement hits... Then comes the guilt, the worry, and before you know it, the cycle starts all over again.

This chapter is about breaking that loop without relying on willpower, but instead with systems and self-awareness.

Story Time!

Meet Brodie.

Brodie paid off *$6,500* in credit card debt over 14 months. He was focused, locked in, and proud of the progress.

But then came his cousin's wedding. He didn't want to show up in old clothes, so he put a new suit on his card.

A month later, his car needed tires. He didn't want to drain his emergency fund, so he charged it.

Then his friends planned a last-minute getaway. "I deserve it," he told himself. Swipe.

By the end of the year, Brodie was back up to $4,200 in credit card debt. This didn't happen because he wasn't smart, it happened because he never built a system to kill temptation. For you, that stops here.

What could Brodie have done differently? What plays could he have made to avoid falling back into debt so hard?

Here are some battle-tested strategies to help you stay out of the cycle of debt:

1. Set a 48-Hour Rule for Purchases Over $100

If it's not urgent or essential, wait 48 hours. Let the emotion pass, and see if you still want it. 9 times out of 10, you won't.

Pro Tip: Make this a rule for your entire household, not just yourself

2. Unsubscribe, Unfollow, and Uninstall

With a computer in your pocket and access to the world at your fingertips, temptation often enters through your phone, not your wallet.

- Unsubscribe from promotional emails
- Unfollow accounts that make you feel "behind"
- Delete shopping apps that lead to mindless spending

Control what you consume, and you'll control what you spend.

3. Use the "Cash-Only Reset" Method

This one is tough, because it's quite easy to justify

using your credit card for the rewards and perks, but desperate times call for desperate measures.

For one month, use only debit or cash.

No credit cards, no Buy Now Pay Later, no "I'll just pay it off later."

This forces you to feel your spending in real time and helps reset impulsive behavior.

4. Name Your No's in Advance

Write down 3–5 common spending traps and your personal policy on them.

We have some examples below:

- Coffee runs → 2x/week max
- Online Purchases → No purchases without it sitting in cart for 24 hours

Naming your no's before the moment of temptation helps you make stronger decisions in the actual moment.

5. Track Emotional Spending Triggers

Keep a record of your impulse purchases. Recommendation: Use the notes app, so it will always be with you.

What were you feeling right before you spent?

What triggered the urge?

Are you starting to notice patterns like stress, boredom, or comparison?

Once you identify the patterns, you can start replacing the habit with something healthier.

Temptation is not a one-size-fits-all. What triggers you will probably be different than what triggers someone else. That's why it helps to have your own temptation killer guide.

Paying off debt gave you more options (freedom). Don't trade that for a hit of dopamine at 22% interest. And no you don't need to avoid spending forever, but you should be spending with intention and not emotion. Protect you peace, and let high-interest debt be a chapter you don't need to go back and rereading over and over again.

CHAPTER 9

Case Study:
$30k in Debt to Debt-Free in 18 Months

When Malik first looked at the numbers, it didn't feel real.

- $11,200 in credit card debt
- $6,000 left on a personal loan
- $12,800 on a car with a "higher than normal" interest rate

He was literally one missed paycheck from disaster.

He wasn't careless... he was surviving, supporting family, covering unexpected costs, and doing what he thought was normal. That is until the minimum payments started adding up to be more than his rent.

He had stress on repeat, every single month. But something clicked the day he opened a credit card statement and saw only $18 of his $150 minimum payment went to the principle. This means the rest went toward interest...

That was the day he built a new plan and stuck to it.

He picked the Snowball Method because he needed fast wins. His first victory was wiping out a $700 balance in one month. He picked up a weekend side hustle tutoring which brought in an extra $400 – $600 per month, putting every penny toward debt.

He paused all non-essentials: no shopping, no new tech, no takeout. Just survival and strategy.

He set a "no swipe rule", freezing his credit cards (literally), and refused to use them unless it was a life-or-death emergency.

He created cash flow clarity and gave every dollar a destination.

In 18 months, he went from $30K in debt to $0.

Consistency, sacrifice, and a clear target.

His biggest shift wasn't the money, it was the mindset. Malik did more than pay off debt, he took back control of his life.

Can you relate?

Maybe your numbers are different, and maybe your situation looks nothing like Malik's, or maybe it looks exactly the same. Either way, if you've ever felt stuck, overwhelmed, or like your money was already spent before it even hit your account... Then you already know the feeling.

And you also know it's time to change it.
Let Malik's story remind you that you don't need a miracle, you need a plan, a reason, and a willingness to stick with it. The next chapter is yours to write.

THIRD PLAY

PLAN FOR RETIREMENT

CHAPTER 10

Master The Retirement Game

Retirement isn't an age. **READ THAT AGAIN!**

Retirement is the point where your money works harder than you do. Where your income no longer depends on your labor. Where you get to choose how you spend your time because you built a lasting foundation. And the part most people miss or avoid is that the earlier you start, the easier it gets.

Let's say you want to retire at 60 and need $1 million to live comfortably. If you start investing at age 25, you can reach that goal by putting aside about $300 per month with a assumed conservative 7% return.

Wait until age 35? Now it's $630/month.

Wait until 45? Try $1,350/month.

That's the power of time and compound interest. It's not just what you save, it's how long it has to grow. The earlier you start, the less you have to contribute. The later you start, the more you have to fight uphill.

Excuses for why people don't plan:

- "I'll save for retirement when I make more."
- "I don't know where to start, so I'll deal with it later."
- "Retirement feels too far away to matter right now."
- "I'm just trying to survive today, so the future can wait."

We know life is expensive and retirement feels like something your "future self" should worry about. But if you get to the root of it, your future self is being built by your current choices. And if you wait until it feels comfortable, it will always be too late.

When you invest in your future, you're doing more than "saving." You're building assets, protecting your future self, and putting money into a system that rewards time, patience, and consistency. You're giving yourself the most valuable currency of all: **FREEDOM!**

Let's take a look at what planning for retirement means:

- You won't be forced to work a job you hate just to survive
- You can take care of your health, family, and peace of mind
- You get to make choices based on what's best, not just what's urgent

Planning for retirement is you building power and protection.

Over the next few chapters, we will break down the different retirement tools you have at your disposal. You'll learn how to "inflation-proof" your future, and make your retirement goals attainable. By the end of the third play, you will have created a retirement strategy that you can be proud of.

You don't need to max out every account, but **start where you are right now.**

CHAPTER 11

401(k),403(b), IRA? Let's Break It Down

By now, you know that retirement is a "when you have enough", not a "when you turn" kind of goal. But to get there, you need to know what vehicles are available and which ones are best for you.

Right now the retirement landscape offers more tools than ever, but most people only hear about the big two: 401(k)/403(b) & Individual Retirement Account (IRA). This chapter breaks it all down, including the lesser-known tools that could quietly accelerate your wealth.

To start, all retirement accounts fall into two tax buckets:

- Traditional (pre-tax) - Contributions are tax deferred meaning you don't pay taxes until later when you withdraw from your retirement.
- Roth (after-tax) - Contributions are tax-exempt meaning you pay taxes now. Roth also means tax free growth and tax free withdrawals.

The main difference is when you pay the IRS. Simply put, a traditional account helps you now and a Roth helps you later. We'll help you decide which is right for your situation a bit later. First, let's go over some of the different retirement accounts that are available to you, and how you can maximize your investments.

401(k) and 403(b)

Employer-Sponsored Plans

- Who it's for:
  - Employees at companies or nonprofits
- 2025 contribution limit:
  - $23,000 annually if under 50
  - $30,500 with catch-up if 50 or older
- Tax advantage:
  - Traditional 401(k) = tax-deductible now
  - Roth 401(k) = grows tax-free

These are workhorse accounts that can potentially score you free money, if managed correctly. We will talk about employer matching in the next chapter. And for clarification, here is the difference between a 401(k) and a 403(b).

401(k) = for "for profit" companies
403(b) = for "nonprofit" companies

So which one is right for you? If you will be making more money now, than in retirement, traditional might make more sense. If you're starting to invest early and plan to have large disbursements from investments and retirement, then Roth could be the smarter play.

IRA (Individual Retirement Account)

The "Do it Yourself (DIY)" Retirement Account

- Who it's for:
  - Anyone with earned income
- 2025 contribution limit:
  - $7,000 per year if under 50
  - $8,000 if 50 or older
- Types/Tax Advantages:
  - Traditional IRA: tax deductible today; taxed on withdrawals
  - Roth IRA: taxed today; tax-free withdrawals
    - Income limits apply for Roth IRA contributions based on your Modified Adjusted Gross Income (MAGI)
      - **Full contribution**: If your MAGI is less than $150,000, you can contribute the full amount ($7,000, or $8,000 if 50 or older).
      - **Partial contribution**: If your MAGI is between $150,000 and $165,000, your contribution limit is reduced.
      - **No contribution**: If your MAGI is $165,000 or more, you are not eligible to contribute directly to a Roth IRA.

IRAs are perfect if your job doesn't offer a 401(k)/403(b) or if you want to save in addition to one. Many people do both: 401(k) through work + Roth IRA on their own.

■ Use an IRA to start investing even if your job doesn't offer a plan.
■ Use a Roth IRA if you want tax-free withdrawals in retirement.

Lesser-Known, But Powerful Retirement Accounts

Simplified Employee Pension (SEP IRA)

- Who it's for:
  - Freelancers, side hustlers, and small business owners
- 2025 contribution limit:
  - Up to 25% of net income, capped at $69,000
- Advantages:
  - Easy to set up
  - Contributions are tax-deductible
  - No Roth version yet

■ SEP IRA's are a great way for small business owners to start planning for retirement and lower their taxable income.

Savings Incentive Match Plan for Employees (Simple IRA)

- Who it's for:
  - Small business owners with fewer than 100 employees
- 2025 contribution limit:
  - $16,000
- Advantages:
  - Easier and cheaper to set up and administer than a 401(k)

■ Simple IRA's are great for business owners who want to offer retirement plans without the big cost of a full 401(k).

Self-Directed IRA (SDIRA)

- Who it's for:
  - Investors who want more control over their retirement funds
- 2025 contribution limit:
  - $7,000 per year if under 50
  - $8,000 if 50 or older
- Advantages:
  - Can invest retirement funds in more than stock market securities
    - Able to invest in real estate, private companies, digital assets (crypto), and much more

■ Self-directed IRA's are for experienced investors who want to diversify outside the stock market using retirement funds

SDIRAs come with risk and regulations. Know the rules before diving into this type of retirement account.

Health Savings Account (HSA) - The Hidden Retirement Account

- Who it's for:
  - Anyone with a high-deductible health plan and is contributing funds to a Health Savings Account.
- 2025 contribution limit:
  - $4,300 for individuals
  - $8,550 for families

- Advantages:
    - Triple Tax Break
        - Contributions are tax-deductible
        - Grows tax-free
        - Withdrawals are tax-free if used for qualified medical expenses
    - Once you turn 65, you can withdraw HSA funds for anything, and it essentially acts like a traditional IRA

■ HSA's are great for staking tax-free money while covering future medical costs in retirement

Whew! That is a lot of retirement accounts. So the next question is, which one should you start with? Remember what we said earlier? **Start where you are.**

If your employer offers a match:

- Contribute to your 401(k) up to the match first
- Then max out a Roth IRA (if income limits allow)
- Go back and contribute more to your 401(k) if you still have room

If you're self-employed:

- Open a SEP IRA or Solo 401(k) (if you want higher contribution limits)
- Use a Roth IRA for personal investing
- Consider a Self-Directed IRA if you're a more advanced investor

A final thought before going to the next topic:

Each dollar you put into a retirement account is doing two things at once:

1. It's building your future income
2. It's buying back your future freedom

You're creating the option to walk away, pivot, or pause when life calls for it. The key is to start, even if it's just $50 a month. And don't finish this chapter telling yourself "it's too late for me." Start right now, and let time do what time does best: Grow, then eventually multiply the seeds that you are planting today.

RETIREMENT ACCOUNTS COMPARISON

ACCOUNT	WHO IT'S FOR	2025 CONTRIBUTION LIMIT	KEY FEATURES
401(K) / 403(B)	employees with a plan at work	\$23,000 + match \$30,500 if 50+	Potential employer match
IRA	anyone with earned income	\$7,000 \$8,000 if 50+	Traditional or Roth
SEP IRA	self-employed, side hustles	Higher limit than a regular IRA	Higher limit than a regular IRA
SIMPLE IRA	small businesses (1-100 employees)	\$16,000	Easier set up than a 401(k)
SELF-DIRECTED IRA	advanced investors	\$7,000 \$8,000 if 50+	Wider investment choice
HSA	with a high-deductible health plan	\$4,300 \$8,550 for families	Triple tax advantage *

CHAPTER 12

Employer Match = Free Money

If your employer offers a 401(k) or 403(b) with a match, congratulations! You're being offered free money. Let's break down what an employer match is without complicating it.

When you contribute to your retirement plan, your employer agrees to match a portion of what you put in. It might look like this:

"We'll match 100% of the first 4% of your salary that you contribute."

That means if you earn $60,000 and contribute 4% ($2,400/year), your employer will also contribute $2,400... for free.

That's a 100% return on your money... instantly!

Skipping your match is like saying no to a raise. If you're just getting started or feel like it's a small amount, it matters. This is money you don't have to earn, hustle for, or wait on. All you have to do is participate.

Every employer is different and has different brokerages they use. The first thing you need to do is log into your 401(k) or 403(b) portal (contact HR if you're unsure where to go).

Once logged in, you need to set your contribution percentage to at least the amount that gets you the maximum match amount (HR can explain those numbers to you). This is where you also choose where your contributions will go, either Roth or Traditional (we broke those down earlier). And you're done! Your employer handles the rest.

**Pro Tip: Your employer's contribution doesn't count toward your personal limit. It's on top.*

Quick Real-World Example:

- Salary: $70,000
- Employer match: 100% of the first 5%
- You contribute: $3,500
- Employer contributes: $3,500
- Total retirement savings that year? $7,000

You just doubled your contribution without lifting a finger.

An employer match...

- Accelerates your retirement savings
- Builds the habit of investing consistently
- Reduces how much of your own money you need to hit your goals
- Proves that small moves stack up fast

You can't control the market, but you can control whether you say yes to free money. Don't leave it on the table. Get the match, build the habit, stack your freedom!

Quick Tutorial: How to Set Up Your Employer Match

1. Log into your 401(k) or 403(b) portal. (Ask your HR or benefits team, if you don't know where to go.)
2. Set your contribution percentage to at least the amount your employer will match. (Usually between 4 – 6% of your paycheck.)
3. Choose your tax type: Roth or Traditional. (We explained both earlier. choose based on your current vs. future tax expectations.)
4. Save your changes. That's it.
5. Your employer automatically adds the match to your retirement account as you contribute.

You don't have to do anything else but contribute consistently and let the system work for you.

CHAPTER 13

Roth vs. Traditional: Choose Your Tax Strategy

Before we go any further, let's make something clear:

We are not tax advisors.

This chapter and book are for educational purposes only. Everyone's financial and tax situation are different. For personalized advice, you should speak with a certified tax professional before making your final decision.

Now that that's out the way, let's get you the knowledge to ask smarter questions and make informed plays.

What's really the difference between Roth and Traditional retirement accounts? At the core, the difference is when you want to pay taxes.

Traditional Retirement Accounts

With Traditional accounts contributions are made *pre-tax*. This translates to you getting tax breaks today while your money grows tax-deferred (postponing taxes). However, with a traditional account, you will pay taxes on any amount you withdraw during retirement. Good if you expect to be in a lower tax bracket later in life or if you need to reduce taxable income today.

Roth Retirement Accounts

With Roth accounts, contributions are made with after-*tax dollars*. This translates to you paying taxes today and your money growing tax free. You don't receive tax breaks like with a traditional account, but your withdrawals will be tax-free when it's time for retirement. This is great if you are expecting to be in a higher tax bracket later in life. You are also locking in today's tax rate for your long-term growth (no one knows how the tax rate will change in the future).

So which one should you choose? I bet you can guess the answer. It depends on you and your future. But here are some helpful guidelines:

Choose Traditional if:

- You want a tax deduction today
- You need to reduce your taxable income (ex: to qualify for other tax benefits)
- You plan to be in a lower tax bracket in retirement

Choose Roth if:

- You're early in your career (lower income, lower taxes)
- You expect your income and tax rate to go up
- You want tax-free growth and peace of mind in retirement
- You're building wealth for long-term flexibility

An idea is contributing to a Roth 401(k) and a Traditional IRA, the combination is really up to you.

One important thing to note is that the contribution limit is shared between Roth and Traditional IRA's. You **cannot** contribute $7,000 to a Traditional IRA **AND** contribute $7,000 to a Roth IRA. You can split it any way, but the total cap applies to both. Our recommendation is find out which is best for your situation, and choose that one.

For higher earners, there's also a strategy called the Backdoor Roth IRA, where you contribute to a Traditional IRA and convert it to a Roth. This strategy comes with rules and tax implications, so be sure to check with a tax professional before using this play.

And if you've changed jobs, you can roll over your old 401(k) into an IRA or your new employer's plan. Rollovers won't count toward your contribution limits, and they give you more control over your investments.

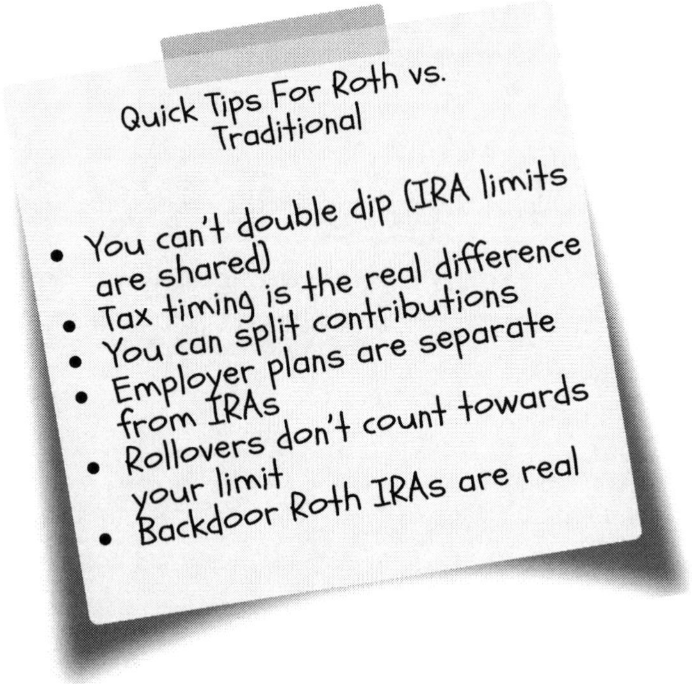

CHAPTER 14

Inflation-Proof Your Future

You're almost done with the third play and have taken steps to invest, grow your retirement accounts, and secure your future. But the reality is that no one can afford to ignore the silent threat of inflation.

The simple fact that a million dollars in the future won't be able to buy what a million buys today. Inflation is the slow, steady increase in process that erodes the value of your money over time. Not planning for this could have you saving for retirement with numbers that don't match reality.

Inflation is the reason why gas that used to cost $2 now costs $4, why groceries feel more expensive every month, and exactly why "future you" will need more money to live the same lifestyle. The historical average for inflation is around 2–3% per year, but as we've seen in recent years, it can spike much higher.

At just 3% inflation, $100 today will be worth only $74 in 10 years. That's why "inflation-proofing" your future is essential. Now let's get into how you can protect you wealth from inflation.

First off, you need to invest and not just save.

Savings accounts are safe, but they rarely outpace inflation.

Your retirement dollars should be invested in assets that grow over time, like stocks, ETFs, real estate, and mutual funds. These assets carry some risk, but they also offer the growth potential needed to beat inflation long-term.

*Remember: Not investing is a risk too because inflation never takes a day off.

Next, you want to use Roth accounts strategically.

Roth IRAs and Roth 401(k)s grow tax-free, and your withdrawals in retirement aren't taxed either. That means if inflation causes prices to rise and taxes to go up, you're protected from both.

You also want to diversify your investments.

Don't put everything in one basket. A diversified portfolio helps you absorb economic shifts, including inflation spikes.

Strong inflation-resistant assets include:

- Stocks
- Real estate
- Treasury Inflation-Protected Securities (TIPS)
- Commodities (like energy, metals, etc.)
- Real Estate Investment Trusts (REITs)

You don't need to own all of these, but knowing how they work gives you tools to adjust your strategy.

As your income grows, increase your contributions.

If you're contributing $200/month to your retirement now, plan to increase that amount every year. Even a 3% – 5% bump annually can make a massive difference over time.

**Treat your contributions like your income and have them grow as you do.*

Plan for a longer and more expensive retirement.

With higher life expectancy, more expensive healthcare, combined with a more active lifestyle, it would be a smart move to assume you'll need more in retirement. Think 25-30 years *after* you expect to retire and plan for that.

Inflation doesn't have to destroy your retirement dreams, but ignoring it has the potential to wreck your plans.

You have to do more than just save for the future, you need to protect it.

You've made it to the end of the Third Play and your money is fueling your retirement future. In the next play, we are going to accelerate your financial freedom journey by diving into long-term passive income.

FOURTH PLAY

INVEST IN LONG-TERM ASSETS

CHAPTER 15

The Investor Mindset

You've made it to the Fourth Play, the turning point for your future. With the last three plays, you laid your foundation, fought your debt, and protected your future. Now it's time to build wealth on purpose.

That begins with one shift:

Stop thinking like a spender, and start thinking like an investor.

In this play, we want to introduce something called *The Investor Mindset*. This isn't about having millions of dollars or picking the next big stock, it's about seeing every dollar as a tool instead of a trophy. Shifting from "How much can I afford to spend?" to "How can I make this grow?"

The Investor Mindset is about thinking long-term, being patient, and staying consistent when everyone else is panicking. It's about moving differently and purposely, because you are building something that will last for generations to come.

If you had to guess why most people never fully adopt *The Investor Mindset,* what would you say? The sad truth is that most people were never taught how. Majority of us were raised on; *"Save your money," "Don't lose it," "Don't take risks."* All important, but also incomplete. We weren't taught how to grow money.

We weren't taught how to buy assets, earn passive income, or understand compound growth. We fear or delay investing until we're "ready," only to dip a toe when we could be making huge strides toward financial freedom. All that changes right now.

Here's what happens when you adopt an investor's mindset:

- You start making decisions based on impact, not impulse
- You become less reactive and more strategic
- You stop "just spending money" and instead assign it jobs
- You train money to work for you

The Investor's Mindset does so much more than change your finances. It changes how you handle stress, promotes positive relationships, increases your confidence, and can lead to you creating a lasting legacy. When you realize you can build wealth intentionally, you stop waiting for life to happen, and start designing it.

You don't need permission to start, but if you're looking for it, WE are giving you that permission right now.

Making six figures isn't a requirement, and you don't have to wait until everything is lined up perfectly. The only requirement is a willingness to learn, move, and stay consistent. And the mindset is just the beginning. In the next chapters we will talk about the kinds of investments that generate passive income, build long-term wealth, and put you on the path to freedom.

CHAPTER 16

Stock Market Basics: Buy, Hold, Build

If you're reading this book, you've probably heard the phrase *"Invest in the stock market"* more than a few times. But has anyone really explained to you how the stock market works? Or why it matters? Let's fix that right now with this chapter being your *101* into the world of stock market investing. We aren't teaching day trading, or uncovering the secret to stock-picking, this is about you becoming a builder. Someone who wants to use the market as a long-term wealth engine.

So, what is the stock market exactly?

At its core, the stock market is a place where companies sell ownership in their business to raise money. Each share of stock represents a tiny slice of that business. This means when you buy a stock, you're not just holding a number on a screen, you own part of a real company.

If the company grows in value, so does your investment. If the company pays dividends, you get a cut. And when millions of people invest in hundreds or thousands of companies, that entire system becomes what we call "the market."

Now that we have a high level definition of the stock market, let's talk about why it works so well.

The U.S. stock market has been one of the most reliable wealth-building tools in history.

See facts below:

- The S&P 500 - an index fund that tracks 500 of the biggest U.S. companies, has returned an average of 10% – 11% per year over the last century.
- Even with market crashes, wars, recessions, and pandemics, the market has consistently rebounded and grown over time.
- If you had invested just $1,000 in the S&P 500 in 1990, and reinvested dividends, that would be worth over $25,000 today.

This is not luck, it's compounded growth mixed with consistency and patience.

**Pro Tip: The market doesn't reward emotion. It rewards time in the game.*

"It's not about timing the market, but about time in the market"

Ok, we defined and proved that the stock market has been a monster of a wealth generator for decades, but how does that translate to YOU making money? There are two basic ways your investments can grow in the stock market. the first is capital appreciation, and the second is dividends.

Capital appreciation happens when the value of a stock you own goes up. For example, you purchase a share of a company for $100, the value of that share grows to $150, that is an appreciation of $50. This is one of the core engines of wealth building in the stock market and understanding it can help you see money as an active tool for growth instead of something that is static.

This form of investing is so powerful because it works while you sleep. You aren't trading time for money, and once you buy the investment, you don't have to do anything else for it to grow. Buying and holding is just the tip of the investing iceberg, as compound interest is the secret weapon that puts your investments into overdrive! (More on that in the Fifth Play).

Remember, we said capital appreciation is the first and most common way to grow money in the stock market. Now we will discuss dividends and the benefits of being a shareholder.

We like to describe dividends as a "thank you" from a company to it's shareholders. When a company earns profits, it has a choice: reinvest that money into the business, or share the profits with its shareholders. The shared profit is called a dividend. Essentially getting paid for owning shares of a company.

A quick example would go something like this:

Let's say you own 100 shares of a company that pays a $1 dividend per share every year. That means you'll receive $100 per year, just for owning the stock. A simple formula, but very effective. Not to mention, the more shares you own (or the more companies you're invested in that pay dividends), the more you collect.

Now this leaves you with two options:

1. Reinvest the Dividends - Use the money to automatically buy more shares
2. Take the Cash - Treat it like passive income

If you're serious about passive income, dividends are one of the most reliable building blocks available. They reward patience, grow with time, and help create cash flow regardless of if you're reinvesting or ready to reap the benefits.

Both capital appreciation and dividends have their benefits, so learning more about both is essential. Also, keep in mind that the stock market is a tool, not a magic trick. It has built wealth for many individuals, but it isn't risk free. Before we leave the fourth play, we will dive deep into risk management and how that is one of the most important aspects of investing.

Ultimately you have to do what makes sense for you and your financial situation. Remember that with stock market investing, you have the ability to do any combination of capital appreciation and dividend investing. Starting with one form now and adding/switch later down the road is pretty common as well. Investing in the stock market leaves much room for flexibility.

With flexibility comes the need to learn many of the terms that are associated with the stock market. We will do our best to go over the most common key terms and tools you'll encounter, but added a cheat sheet at the end of this chapter for you to glance at if you ever need a quick refresher, which will be a great page to bookmark.

Individual Stocks

Represents one specific company in the market, where the value goes up or down based on company performance. Big reward, but also big risk due to lack of diversification.

**Use when you believe in a company long-term and you understand the risks.*

Mutual Funds

A bundle of many stocks or bonds managed by a professional. You buy into the fund and own a portion of every asset inside it. These funds are often actively managed by a fund manager meaning automatic diversification. Due to fund management, mutual funds typically come with fees that are used to pay the fund manager. However, this form of investing is great for beginners who want easy diversification

**Use when you want a hands-off, diversified option, but be aware of fees*

ETFs (Exchange-Traded Funds)

Like mutual funds, but trade like stocks on the market. They are typically paired with lower fees than mutual funds, but provide the instant diversification you might be looking for. A great form of passive diversified investing.

**Use when you want easy diversification and lower fees with more flexibility*

Index Funds

A type of mutual fund or ETF that tracks a market index, like the S&P 500 or the Nasdaq. These funds hold shares of many companies to match the performance of the overall market. Great beginner investment for, great for long-term growth, and very low-maintenance.

**Use when you want reliable, long-term growth without picking individual stocks*

It would take a while to go over every single definition and important word that is involved with the stock market, so we will stop here for now, but will remind you of the goal before going to the next chapter.

Adopt The Investors Mindset. Instead of being driven to buy things that lose value over time (cars, gadgets, clothes), focus on things that gain value over time like stocks and other forms of investments.

The stock market is a long game that you win by staying in. You don't need to be a trader or time the market. You just need to buy quality assets, hold them through the ups and downs, and keep building consistently over time. In the next chapter we will examine another behemoth of wealth generation that has passed the test of time.

STOCK MARKET BASICS GLOSSARY

INDIVIDUAL STOCKS

A single share in a specific company

MUTUAL FUNDS

A managed fund pooling many stocks

ETFs

Funds that trade like individual stocks

REITs

Real estate investment funds

DIVIDENDS

Regular profit-sharing payments

INDEX FUNDS

Funds tracking a market index

BLUE-CHIP STOCKS

Shares in large, established companies

MARKET CORRECTIONS

Market drop of 10% or more

CHAPTER 17

Real Estate: Bricks, Mortgage, and Cash Flow

Being a homeowner is a great first step for anyone on the road to financial freedom. Real estate investing however is more than just owning property. It's more than a house and keys to a front door. Real estate is one of the most powerful wealth-building engines in history. In fact, 90% of millionaires in the U.S. have some kind of real estate in their portfolio. Why? Because it combines cash flow, leverage, appreciation, tax advantages, and control in a way few other assets can. Let's dig in and break down what matters most for first time investors.

Investing in real estate means you're putting your money into property that can make you money in return. This can be either through income, growth, or both.

Here are some basic strategies for real estate investing:

- **Buy and Hold**: You buy a home or unit and rent it out for monthly income. This strategy is probably the most common, because the flexibility of cash flow (more on this later in the chapter)
- **House Flipping**: You buy undervalued property, renovate that property, and sell it for profit
- **REITs**: You invest in companies that own real estate (the stock market version of real estate)

This list is far from all encompassing, but the reason real estate works so well and is so powerful
is because it combines several unique money-making advantages. With real estate, you have in your arsenal the ability to make money many different ways. We listed some of those ways below.

- **Generates Cash Flow**
  - Rental income provides steady, recurring revenue. It's one of the most reliable forms of passive income.
- **Growth and Appreciation**
  - Over time, real estate tends to rise in value. Historically, U.S. home prices have appreciated 3% – 5% annually, depending on the market.
- **Leverage**
  - You can use other people's money (like a mortgage) to control a high-value asset. For example, a 5% down payment gets you 100% of the property's value. (That's the magic of leverage: small capital, big control.)
- **Tax Advantages**
  - Depreciation (on paper losses) can reduce your taxable income.
  - The interest you pay on your mortgage is tax deductible.
  - 1031 exchanges let you sell and reinvest without immediate tax hits
- **Tangible Asset**
  - It's real. It's physical. You can touch it, improve it, sell it, or even live in it. Real estate is one of the few investments that's also a shelter, service, and store of value.

Quick Fact: Between 2000 and 2020, average U.S. home prices rose over 100%. And many real estate investors earn 6–12% returns annually, not including the growth in equity of the home.

So far, real estate sounds like a great form of investment, right? And it is, but before jumping in, let's talk versatility.

Remember when we mentioned the *Buy and Hold* method of investing and its flexibility? Well let's see if these scenarios sound familiar. Have you ever been a renter? Meaning someone owned the place you rented out.

What about AirBnB? Again, the owner is leveraging their property as a short/mid term rental to generate income, but also leaving flexibility to increase price and not be locked into having a tenant with a lease.

What about renting a single room or staying in a multi-unit property? Chances are, the owner is doing what's called house hacking. This allows them to live in their property, while renting out other rooms/units.

Each of these methods are great for cash-flow, and are a combination of stable returns (long-term) all the way to maximizing income (short-term rental). Not to mention the equity gained for simply holding onto an appreciating asset.

More creative real estate strategies and ways to obtain homes will be referenced at the end of this chapter.

However, the most basics way to obtain real estate is to leverage your credit. Your credit score is that magic three-digit number that give you more power than you think. Like most situations, the better your credit score, the more leverage you have when obtaining a mortgage. This provides lower interest rates, lower down-payment requirements, and more options. We dive into credit later, so be ready for that conversation.

Along with your credit score comes the need for capital. Unlike the stock market, which generally requires very little money to get started, purchasing a home using leverage (getting a mortgage) requires you to have cash for a down payment, closing costs, and emergency reserves.

It is also important not to get caught up in speculation. Solely relying on the potential increase in equity shouldn't drive your decision to invest in real estate. Make sure the purchase produces income today.

Always triple check your numbers before following through with a real estate transaction.

To add some clarity, we need to quickly reference some exit strategies that allow flexibility and can help you not feel "stuck".
You could...

- Sell and take profit
- Refinance to pull out equity
- 1031 exchange to defer taxes and upgrade
- Hold forever for cash flow and appreciation

Flexibility is the name of the game with real estate!

Lastly, remember that real estate is a business and with it comes work. Tenants, repairs, management, and at times headaches. Luckily, you don't have to do it all by yourself. Find a team with a proven track record to assist you along the way.

You don't need to have millions in the bank to invest in real estate. You simply need patience, a plan, and a willingness to learn. Start small, start safe, and start thinking like an owner. Real estate is one of the few investments that pays you today, appreciates tomorrow, and can shelter you forever.

REAL ESTATE STRATEGIES

RENTAL PROPERTY

Buy and hold real estate for long-term rental income

SHORT-TERM RENTAL

Rent out properties on platforms like Airbnb for short stays

OUT-OF-STATE REAL ESTATE

Invest in properties in different geographical markets

HOUSE HACKING

Live in one unit of a multi-family home, rent out the rest

BRRRR METHOD

Stands for Buy, Rehab, Rent, Refinance. and Repeat

BUYING FORECLOSURES

Purchase homes in foreclosure at a reduced price

AUCTION SALES

Find and bid on properties available at real estate auctions

CHAPTER 18

Playing Defense: Risk Management

This chapter is going to be the anchor of your investing journey and where we teach you how to protect what you're building. Sadly, risk management is where most people fall short and end up nose diving back to where they started.

Building wealth isn't just about offense, it's also about protecting the plays you're running. When you go all-in without a plan or invest without understanding, it can result in big losses and broken confidence. Also, this chapter is not telling you to play scared, but rather play smart. You've worked hard to get this far, so let's move intentionally and set you up to last.

What is Risk Management exactly? It's defined as the practice of identifying potential losses before they happen and making intentional moves to reduce their impact. With investing, it means knowing what you are investing in and understanding the potential downsides. It means you have proactively put safeguards in place to reduce loss. You won't be able to eliminate all risk, that isn't the goal, but we do want to make sure one mistake won't take you out the game.

It doesn't matter if you're investing in stocks, real estate, or some other form of investing, risk is always part of the equation. But the more you understand the potential risk, the better you can plan for it. Next are some common risks to watch out for:

Market Risk
This is the one most people know. It's when the value of your investment drops and stays down longer than expected. Markets are cyclical, and downturns are normal. The key is staying invested long enough to recover.

Liquidity Risk
Let's say you need money today, but your investment isn't easily converted to cash (like a rental property), so you're stuck. It is good to have liquid savings set aside, just in case.

Credit Risk
This applies when someone owes you money. If a tenant stops paying or a borrower defaults, your expected income disappears. On top of frustrating you, this type of risk can quickly put your finances in a bind.

Emotional Risk
This is the silent killer. Panic-selling during a market dip, chasing hype, or taking your money out too soon can sabotage long-term growth. Remember that discipline beats emotion every time.

Again, the goal isn't to avoid risk completely, the goal is to make sure you understand and are prepared for the potential risks that may arise. Real investors plan and adjust when necessary. Now let's get into some strategies that provide a solid defense and assist with risk management.

1. Diversification
Don't put all your eggs in one basket. Spread your investments across different asset classes (stocks, real estate, cash, business) and even within each class (like ETFs instead of just one stock).

2. Keep Emergency Cash
We talked about this earlier in the book, but it doesn't hurt to mention it again. You'll want to keep at least 3 – 6 months of living expenses for emergencies.

3. Know Your Timeline
If you need money in the next 12 months, it shouldn't be in stocks. Match your investment to your timeline. If you have short-term goals then you want to lean towards safer options. Long-term investments have more room for growth and provide you with time to recover in case things go sideways for a while.

4. Don't Use Money You Can't Afford to Lose
Never gamble rent money on the market. Never max out a credit card on "the perfect real estate deal." Invest from overflow and abundance instead of investing out of desperation.

5. Stay Educated
Risk shrinks the more you understand what you're doing. Keep learning, and if you uncover a winning strategy, repeat until it stops working for you. Confidence comes from clarity.

6. Use Exit Strategies

Always ask: "If this goes wrong, what's my backup plan?" Have multiple paths:

- Sell it
- Rent it
- Refinance it
- Pause and rebuild

A smart investor plans for the worst and still moves confidently. Risk should not be a wall that causes you to stand still or turn around. It should be a speed bump that promotes you to slow down, because moving too fast in this area could cause damage. Protect yourself and your wealth from uncertainty.

FIFTH PLAY

STRATEGIC WEALTH BUILDING

CHAPTER 19

Automation: The Silent Wealth Machine

By now, you've checked your financial mindset, paid down some heavy high-interest debt, set yourself up for retirement, and started investing in long-term assets. You've built some true momentum. But now it's time to elevate everything you've learned so far with next level strategies and tools.

Welcome to The Fifth Play, where we discover the meaning of working smarter and not harder. It is time to transition that momentum into true mastery. To kick off this play, we are going to introduce the secret wealth building machine: Automation.

Most people rely on memory, willpower, or good intentions to always be present while achieving goals. That just isn't going to happen. We forget things and lose motivation all the time. Relying on these will ultimately lead most to fail financially. This is where automation comes in.

Automation turns your goals into systems. It removes the human aspect of hesitation, guilt, or friction. It moves while you continue to live your life, and it doesn't get tired or bored. It is the embodiment of consistency that builds wealth in the background. And if you're wondering what tasks can be automated, our answer... **ANYTHING!**

You don't need to micromanage your money to be successful with it. In this chapter, we will walk you through four areas that you can automate right now to create a financial system that builds itself. When your money moves automatically towards your goals, you remove emotion from the equation and turn wealth-building into a well oiled machine.

If you are in a role that provides consistent income, chances are you're receiving your paycheck via direct deposit. Did you know that most employers allow you to split your paycheck into multiple accounts? This method of automation is proactive and moves your money before you receive it. An example of dividing your paycheck is below:

- 75% to Checking (day-to-day expenses)
- 15% to Savings (emergency fund, big goals)
- 10% to Investments (IRA, brokerage, etc.)

Of course you have to make your own decision and use percentages that make sense to you and your situation. You could be building up your emergency fund, starting your investment journey, or maybe you just want to split it up between different checking accounts for money management purposes. The takeaway here is that you have the power to automate your money before it even gets to you.

Next, we will talk about one of our favorite forms of automation, and that is recurring investments. This one action is what separates casual savers and consistent investors. Automating your investments is like paying your future self every week or every month. The frequency is up to you.

We already talked about retirement contributions and employer matching, but beyond automatic investments in your retirement account, you can automate your investments into your individual brokerage account too. This happens in two steps: First you would automate a deposit from your checking into your brokerage account. The next step is choosing which asset you want to purchase using the recurring funds hitting your brokerage account. The most popular brokerages (Fidelity, Charles Schwab, Robinhood, etc.) make this extremely easy.

Use automation to invest a fixed amount of money at regular intervals overtime regardless of what the market is doing. This method of investing is called Dollar-Cost Averaging. When prices are high, the money buys fewer shares, and when prices are low, your money buys more. The purpose is to smooth out the price you pay and reduce that emotional risk we mentioned in the fourth play. Remember that we aren't looking to time the market, we want our time in the market to speak for itself.

Another form of financial automation, is scheduling transfers. This method is similar to income splits, but the money is moving *after* it has hit your checking account. Setting your bank to automatically move money each week or each month is wealth planning at its finest. Emergency fund, home repair fund, travel fund, it doesn't matter. What's important is that once it's setup, you don't have to remember. Overtime, those small transfers stack into big momentum.

The fourth and final form of automation that we will mention is automatically paying your bills and your debts. No one likes to give money away, but it happens far too often with late fees and missed payments. Automatically paying these will keep your credit score healthy and your stress levels low. You can automate your rent/mortgage payment, student loans, utilities, car payment, and even your credit card minimum.

**Pro Tip: Combine this with the debt payment methods mentioned in the second play, and you will be set.*

This list is not all encompassing, but serves as a great spot to start using the "wealth machine" that is automation. Every dollar you automate is a decision you've already made toward freedom. The money is going to be moving anyway, automation helps it move with purpose.

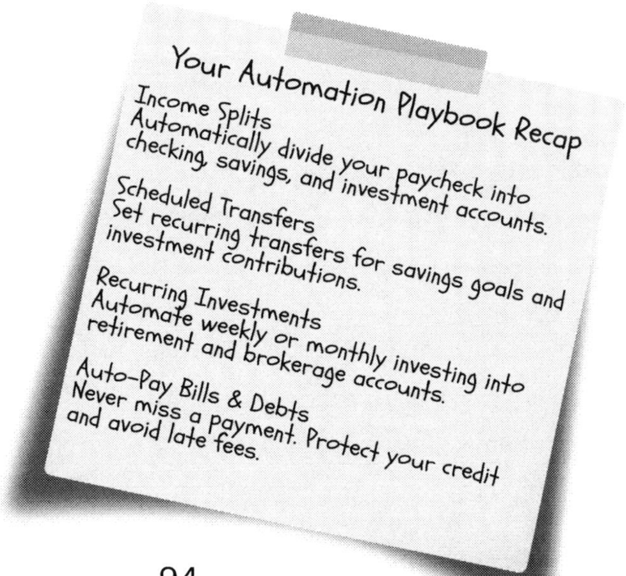

CHAPTER 20

Leveraging Good Debt: The Secret to Scaling Smart

It has to be said... we've been taught to fear debt, and for the most part that fear is justified. High-interest credit cards, payday loans, and emotional spending habits trap people instead of free them. But debt isn't the enemy... bad debt is. Good debt? That is called leverage, a tool the wealthy use every single day.

Good debt is low interest debt (Interest rate under 10%), and can be leveraged to grow your net worth, generate more income, or buy back your time. It's debt that has a clear Return on Investment (ROI) and aligns with your long-term wealth strategy. Specifically, you want to use low-interest debt (good debt) to buy into investments that will yield a greater return than you are losing in interest from the low-interest loan.

We've talked about some of the ways people are using good debt, but let's go through the list:

Real Estate Investing
The most common and powerful form of good debt. You borrow from the bank to buy a property, but you get a tenant that pays the mortgage. And the entire time, you the equity is building from the appreciation of the homes, and each payment that is coming from the tenant. A next level, move is leveraging good debt to purchasing a multi-unit property and begin house

hacking. Using something like an FHA loan, you could do this with a down-payment as low as 3.5%, essentially allowing you to live in your home for free while building equity and gaining experience as a home owner/landlord.

Strategic Education & Certifications

No shame, but not all degrees are worth the price. However, the right education can 10x your income. If a certification, license, or program directly increases your skillset, income, or business capacity, then financing it might be a calculated risk worth taking.

Using Leverage to Keep Cash on Hand

Cash is king, more specifically cash flow is king. There might be a time were using good debt to free up liquidity makes sense. Just remember that it's best to only buy things you can afford, and if you are still paying down high-interest debt, adding more debt (even good debt), could set you back further. Thant bring me to the next purposeful way to leverage good debt.

Using Good Debt to Pay Down Bad Debt

This might sound backward, but in some cases you can use good debt to get rid of bad debt.

Here's how it works:

You take a low-interest loan or line of credit and use it to pay off high-interest debt, like credit cards or payday loans. You're not increasing your total debt, you're just swapping expensive debt for smarter debt. some examples are going to be on the next page.

- 0% APR balance transfer credit card
  - Move high-interest credit card debt onto a card with a 0% promotional introductory rate.
  - If you pay this card off within the promo window (usually 12–18 months), you can save hundreds, or even thousands on what you would have spent on interest.

- Personal loan with low interest
  - Use a fixed-rate loan from a credit union, online lender, or bank to consolidate credit card balances into one manageable monthly payment that typically has a much lower interest rate than any credit card.

- Home equity loan or line of credit (HELOC)
  - If you have equity in your home, you can borrow against it at a much lower rate than your bad debt. Just remember that your home is on the line, so this strategy requires discipline.

These strategies can alleviate some of the pain with high interest, but can bite you twice as hard if you don't stick to a plan. This means don't rack the balance back up on your credit cards. The debt isn't gone, it's only repositioned, and still has to be dealt with.

Good debt sounds great, right? Well before you start applying for 0% interest credit cards and low-interest personal loans, understand that good debt is only "good" if the terms are in you favor. Lenders, banks, and credit card companies all use a similar method to determine how favorable the terms of your borrowed money will be. That #1 thing is your credit score.

A better score = a lower interest rate = more money left in your pocket.

We aren't going to dive too deep into credit scores in this chapter, but it's coming up very soon. Just remember to check your score prior to performing any of the methods listed in this chapter.

CHAPTER 21

Credit As A Tool:
Your Score, Your Strategy, Your Power

If good debt is your silent weapon, then your credit is the ammunition. And while most people see it as a limit, a burden, or even a scam, those who understand it know the truth:

Credit is a tool. Not just for buying things, but for unlocking opportunity.

Buying a home, securing business funding, and lowering your interest rates or insurance premiums all depend on your credit score. It is one of the most powerful tools you have in your financial arsenal, so knowing how to use it is key.

First, what is a credit score and why should you care? Your credit score is a three-digit number that tells lenders, banks, and even landlords how trustworthy you are with borrowed money. It's calculated based on the data in your credit report, and it follows you like a financial resume. Some people think it's random, others think it's rigged, but those that know understand it is formula based, which makes it controllable.

That's correct, your credit score is simply calculated based on your financial decisions, which means you control if it goes up or down. The next question you should be asking is "How is my credit score calculated?" Great question, let's breakdown how the three credit bureaus calculate your magic number.

Category	Impact
Payment History	35%
Credit Utilization	30%
Length of Credit History	15%
Credit Mix	10%
New Credit/Inquiries	10%

Let's unpack these really quick:

- **Payment History (35%)**
  - Are you paying your bills on time, every time?
- **Credit Utilization (30%)**
  - How much of your credit are you using compared to what's available? Under 30% is ideal, but under 10% is **elite**.
- **Length of Credit History (15%)**
  - The longer your accounts have been open, the better. Don't close old cards if you don't have to.
- **Credit Mix (10%)**
  - A healthy blend of credit types (credit cards, auto loans, student loans, mortgage) shows you can manage different kinds of debt.
- **New Credit (10%)**
  - Hard inquiries and newly opened accounts can temporarily lower your score. Too many at once? That's a bad look.

Now that we know how they calculate your credit score, we need to talk about strategies to build or repair your credit. First and foremost, avoid the "fix your credit overnight" trap. If someone tells you they can fix your credit in 48 hours, Run! Real credit repair takes time, discipline, and an actual strategy. Don't fall for shady tricks that sweep your file, they will more than likely backfire. A better path is to build credit the real way: through consistency and control.

Strategies to Build & Repair Your Credit

1. Always Pay Everything On Time

It's not glamorous, but it's the biggest factor.
Late payments can drop your score by 50 – 100 points.
Set up auto-pay or reminders to stay on track.

2. Keep Your Utilization Low

Use less than 30% of your available credit, at most. Use less that 10% if you can. Got a $5,000 limit? Keep your balance under $500 for optimal impact. And if possible, pay off your balance before the statement date (not just the due date). The statement date is when banks submit their report to the bureaus.

3. Don't Close Old Accounts

Unless they're charging high fees, keep your oldest credit lines open. Age matters, and old accounts help establish stability.

4. Use a Secured Credit Card (If You're Rebuilding)

If you're starting from scratch or recovering from damage, a secured credit card (backed by a deposit) is a great way to build or rebuild. These cards don't depend on your credit score, so they are easier to obtain. You would use it just like cash or a debit card. Pay it off monthly and watch your score rise.

5. Ask for Credit Limit Increases
If your score is decent, you can request higher credit limits without a hard inquiry in many cases.
This helps your utilization ratio and shows lenders you can be trusted with a higher credit limit.

6. Check Your Credit Reports Regularly
You're legally entitled to one free credit report per year from each of the three bureaus. Use the website listed below (the only website authorized by federal law to provide consumers with free annual credit reports from each of the three major credit bureaus) to obtain a copy of your credit report.

annualcreditreport.com

Review it for errors, outdated info, or fraud. Dispute anything that doesn't belong.

Credit is about access, and it's more than just a number. It opens doors and opportunities. Protect it, build it, and leverage it strategically, so that it can assist you with reaching financial freedom.

THE CREDIT BUREAUS

EXPERIAN

Focuses on credit utilization and hard inquiries.

EQUIFAX

Emphasizes credit mix and payment history

TRANSUNION

Highlights accounts in collection and credit age

CHAPTER 22

Opportunity Cost: The Hidden Price of Decisions

Every time you spend money, you're making a choice. This choice is not only you deciding what you are buying, it's also deciding what you are not buying with the money you just spent. That unseen choice is called opportunity cost. Often overlooked, opportunity cost is a powerful force in regards to your personal finances.

The value of "the next best thing" you could have done with your money is the best way to describe opportunity cost. For example, you spend $100 on takeout every weekend. That same $100 could have gone into an index fund and grown overtime. The opportunity cost isn't just the $100, it's the future value of that $100. No receipt, or gentle tap on the shoulder, just the silent cost of a missed opportunity.

Let's take this *opportunity* to present a real-world scenario. Imagine you spend $250/month on things that aren't emergencies or priorities. Now imagine, instead you invested that $250/month into a basic index fund that returns 8% annually. here's what that looks like over time:

- After 5 years: $18,369
- After 10 years: $45,609
- After 20 years: $147,801

Now ask yourself this question:

"Was the casual spending really worth a six-figure future?"

And before you say we're telling you not to enjoy your hard earned money, that's not true either. We just want you to know what your decision could be costing you. We want you to start thinking about the cost of opportunities that occur when you're swiping your card. When you're about to make a non-essential purchase, ask yourself:

"Is this worth what I'm giving up long-term?"
"Can this purchase help me build my future?"

If the answer is a clear yes, great, proceed with completing the purchase. But if it is not a resounding yes, then consider holding off for now, or find a way to redirect that money toward a goal that really matters.

When you understand opportunity cost, you will begin to experience a mindset shift that will set you up for success. It's time to start thinking in years, rather than days.

CHAPTER 23

The Wealth Snowball: The Compound Effect in Action

What would you say is the most difficult task when it comes to building wealth? Is it the math behind the numbers? The planning? The lack of motivation? We've learned that it isn't any of those at all. The most difficult part of building wealth is staying committed, even when the results don't show up right away.

You save money, invest, and say no to things that look fun. You take little steps for a while, but it feels like you're barely moving. That's because you haven't hit the curve yet. You haven't seen the part where everything you've done starts working together. That's the moment when all the small moves begin to turn into something powerful.

That's the wealth snowball (not to get confused with the debt snowball strategy), or better known as *The Compound Effect.*

The principle of the compound effect states that **small, consistent actions over time create massive, exponential results.** At first the progress is invisible.

A $25 investment.
Paying $50 towards debt.
A 7-point boost in your credit score.
No one claps. Nothing "big" changes.

But that's ok. The beginning is supposed to feel small. The compound effect isn't something you feel right away. In the early stages, it's slow and boring. You might even convince yourself that what you're doing isn't working, and decide to give up. We've all been there. But the compound effect doesn't reward excitement, it rewards consistency.

Let's look at some numbers that represent the compound effect in action.

Say you invest just $300 a month into an index fund earning a modest 8% return. Not a ton of money, but check out the returns over time.

- After 1 year: $3,700
- After 5 years: $22,000
- After 10 years: $55,000
- After 20 years: $148,000
- After 30 years: $340,000
- After 40 years: $832,000

That $300/month adds up to $144,000 total out of pocket over 40 years... But thanks to compounded growth, it becomes more than $800,000. This is consistency, discipline, and time at work.

And here's a bonus! the compound effect doesn't just stop at your finances, it shows up pretty much everywhere.

Work out 3x a week, and you will have a transformed body in 12 months. Learning one new skill a quarter can transform how you generate income for life. Each action is like a grain of sand or a drop of water. It may be small on its own, but combined with consistency over time, it becomes a desert or the ocean! Or at least a large sand box and a backyard pool.

Let's take some of the skills we learned, and see how they connect to the compound effect.

Automating your savings and investments on a regular basis is an easy way to engage the compound effect. You turn on the machine, and it does the work for you.

Understanding opportunity cost and consciously saying no to what doesn't get you to your goal. Redirecting those funds into investments where they can compound, will make a huge difference over time.

Managing debt and increasing your credit score provides you with opportunities that were once out of your reach. Leverage is just one of the many forms of wealth creation, and consistently making positive financial decisions is the best way to get on the good side of the credit bureaus.

Sprinting your way to financial freedom might work for some, but it rarely pans out the way they hope. Without education, systems, or a rhythm, that wealth can disappear just as fast..

Instill the compound effect, and one day you'll look up and realize the wealth snowball is rolling on it's own!

SIXTH PLAY

PROTECT YOUR ASSETS AND YOUR LEGACY

CHAPTER 24

Insurance:
Protecting The Treasure

Here we are at the final play! Welcome to The Sixth Play. By now, you've built a wealthy mindset, crushed some debt, planned for the future, and added some strategic tools to your tool belt. You've created strong offense, but now it's time to talk about defense. This play is all about playing like a pro by building a fortress around what you've created. That defense starts with a not so exciting, but very crucial topic of the wealth strategy, and that is insurance.

First, a quick reminder:
The information in this chapter and throughout this book is for educational purposes only. Always consult with a certified insurance or financial professional before making personal coverage decisions.

With that being said, let's break it down.

To describe insurance plainly, it is your financial shield. In most cases, you pay a premium to a company who agrees to step in and absorb a big financial blow, so that you don't have to face it alone. This is pretty far from exciting, but can be the difference between a minor setback and a financial collapse.

The next page goes over some of the core insurances that help protect your wealth.

Health Insurance:

A single medical emergency can wipe out years of savings. Whether it's through your employer, the insurance marketplace, or a private plan, make sure you have adequate coverage for:

- Major medical events
- Prescription drugs
- Emergency care

If you're young and healthy, (less trips to the doctor) look into high-deductible plans that allow you to build an HSA (Health Savings Account). That's money for the future potential tax advantages. (We went over HSA's in chapter 11, if you need a refresher).

Auto Insurance:

This one is simple. If you drive, you need coverage. And though settling for liability might look enticing, you might want to consider what's at stake. Beyond liability insurance, look into the following:

- Collision Insurance: Covers damage to your car
- Comprehensive Insurance: Covers theft, weather damage, etc.
- Uninsured motorist: If someone hits you and they don't have insurance

We can't control other drivers, and we can't predict the future, so don't just go for the cheapest plan if you can help it. Go for the plan that protects your net worth in case something goes wrong.

Homeowners Insurance or Renters Insurance:
It doesn't matter if you own or rent, you need to protect your items and your property.

- Homeowners insurance covers the structure and your belongings
- Renters insurance covers your belongings and personal liability

Both are extremely important and give a peace of mind in the unfortunate event of a disaster. Individuals with a wealthy mindset don't just think about the worst case scenario, they prepare for it.

Life Insurance:
If you have children, a spouse, aging parents, or anyone who depends on your income, life insurance is not optional. If something happens to you tomorrow, could your family keep the house? Would they be able to pay the bills? Cover funeral expenses? Or maintain the lifestyle you worked so hard to help them build?

Life insurance is "love" in financial form. It says, "Even if I'm not here, I've still got you."

Choosing life insurance might seem daunting, but luckily you have this playbook to shed some light on a couple of the options for you. People can choose between two main types of life insurance; *Term Life Insurance, and Permanent Life Insurance/Whole Life Insurance.* Whole Life Insurance can be further broken down (Universal Life Insurance, Variable Life Insurance, Guaranteed Universal Life Insurance (GUL)), but we will keep it simple and go over the two main types.

Term Life Insurance - Simple, Affordable, Effective: This type of life insurance covers you for a specific period of time (like 10, 20, or 30 years). If you pass away during that term, your beneficiary gets the payout. This payout is often hundreds of thousands (or even millions) of dollars, and also tax-free.

People lean towards term life insurance because it is significantly cheaper than whole life insurance. It's also pretty straightforward and easy to understand. However, it's important to know that term life insurance is temporary. If you outlive the term, the policy ends and your beneficiaries get nothing. Think of it as renters insurance, and when your "lease" (coverage term) is up, you lose access to the benefits. That is unless you renew, which historically tends to be at a much higher rate, since you are older or may have developed new health conditions.

Also, unlike whole life insurance, term life holds no cash value. There's no saving or investment component when covered under term life. There is no borrowing from it or cashing it out while you are still living. If you don't use it, you lose it. Term life isn't a bank account, it's simply protection.

Whole Life Insurance - Insurance + Investment: This form of insurance lasts your entire life and includes a cash value component that grows over time. People consider this form of insurance because they want coverage that lasts forever. They also like the /saving/investing component. Lastly, most whole life insurance policies will stack your premium payments, allowing you to cash out after a certain amount of time has passed. Just make sure you don't miss any payments.

This sounds like an easy win-win right? It can be, as long as you can afford the premium payments. Whole life insurance is much more expensive than term life insurance. And yes, the money is invested, but can grow pretty slow as well, and have additional fees for cashing out. This is often pitched as an investment strategy, and while it might work for some, it rarely performs better than the overall market.

So which one should you choose? We will leave that answer up to you. Both have benefits and drawbacks. The takeaway is to not look at life insurance as betting on tragedy. This is another defense mechanism that protects the ones you love, giving them more than money. It can also give them time, space, and peace.

Disability Insurance:
If you couldn't work tomorrow, how would your bills get paid? Disability insurance replaces a portion of your income if an illness or injury takes you out of commission.

This is a reminder that we cannot predict the future and that even a short-term disability can create long-term debt. This is the defense for those situations.

Most people don't realize that life situations like hospital bills, injuries, lawsuits, home damages, and untimely deaths can wreck everything they've worked hard to build. Strategically place your financial safety nets in places that make sense. Here are some tips to help you strategize:

- Shop around annually, because prices and policies change all the time.
- Bundle insurances for discounts (auto + renters or home)
- Know your deductibles and understand that a lower monthly premium means higher out-of-pocket costs
- Update your coverage as your wealth grows
- Always keep good records in the event of a claim. (Remember that documentation is your best friend)

The same way any team needs a solid defensive strategy, your wealth needs protection too. You didn't get this far and do all this work just to lose it to one bad day, accident, or unexpected curveball. Guard your assets.

CHAPTER 25

Estate Planning:
Will, Trusts, and Power of Attorney

Most people think estate planning is for the rich. Millionaires, celebrities, or people with mansions and massive investment accounts. But if you have a family, a bank account, or even a favorite watch, then you have an estate.

Estate planning isn't just about death, it's about direction and defines how you stay in control, even when you're no longer able to speak for yourself. So no matter your age, income, or net worth, this chapter matters, because if you don't decide where your assets go, then the state will for you. We've seen too many cases where mourning is followed by confusion and arguments. Believe us when we say, you want the choice to be yours.

Estate planning is the process of organizing your affairs and documenting your wishes so that your assets are distributed exactly how you intend for them to be distributed. It ensures your loved ones are protected from confusion, internal and external conflict, and dismisses court delays. It also allows you to place the people you trust the most in control if you are unable to make any decisions. Having an estate plan is like having peace of mind in the form of a document. Let's dive into the aspects of estate planning.

First up is your will. This is a legal document that outlines who gets what when you die. With a will, you can:

- Name beneficiaries for your assets (money, property, belongings)
- Choose guardians for your children
- Appoint someone (an "executor") to carry out your wishes

What happens if you pass and don't have a will in place? Your estate goes through probate, which is a lengthy, very public, and often expensive legal process. This could leave your family fighting for the assets that you built. A will puts your voice on record, and states exactly what you would like to happen when your time comes.

**Pro Tip: A will can be updated at any time, so it is extremely important to make changes for life events (new child, divorce, remarry, additional assets).*

Next, let's talk about trusts. A trust is a legal entity that holds your assets and distributes them according to the rules you create. Similar to a will, trusts are used to give direction to your assets and give you additional control and protection. Some of the reasons why you would use a trust would be to:

- Avoid probate - assets pass directly to your heirs
- Add conditions - like "my child gets access at age 25"
- Keep things private - unlike wills, trusts aren't public
- Protect assets - from lawsuits or mismanagement

There are many types of trusts, but the two most common types are revocable and irrevocable trusts. As the names imply, one can be updated and the other cannot, except under very rare circumstances.

The bottom line is trusts give you an additional layer of protection, and they are not just for the super rich. We recommend speaking to an estate planning attorney to find out what type of trust would be best for your goals.

We talked about getting your affairs in order for when you pass, but what happens if you're alive but can't make decisions? That is where your "Power of Attorney" (POA) comes in. POA comes in two main flavors: Financial POA and a Medical POA.

A Financial POA gives an agent the authority to manage your financial, legal, and business affairs. The primary purpose is to appoint someone you trust to handle your finances and business matters if you cannot. They are typically granted the ability to manage your bank accounts, pay bills, sign contracts, and process business transactions.

A Medical POA grants someone the power to make medical and health care decisions for you when you are unable to do so yourself. This can be anything from decisions about surgeries and medications to end-of-life care. Unlike a Financial POA, this power can be granted only after a doctor certifies that you are incapacitated and can no longer make health care decisions on your own.

Selecting someone to be your Financial and Medical POA is a big decision; one that involves you choosing someone you trust to speak for you. Without this in place, the hospital or the court system will make this decision for you. Clarity from you to your loved ones is the message here (especially during the tough times).

Accidents happen, and illness strikes without warning. When it does, you want to make sure your family is taken care of, and your money goes to the right people. Estate planning is a “love letter” to your loved ones that survive you. It protects your peace, your people, and your power.

So before we move on, let’s make sure we go over the Estate Planning checklist:

Here’s what you can tackle first:

- Create or update your will
- Consider a trust (talk to a professional)
- Name your financial + medical “Power of Attorney”
- Double-check all your beneficiaries
- Store your documents securely and let someone know where they are
- Revisit your plan every few years

When it comes to estate planning, working with a certified estate attorney is worth every penny. They will make sure your plan is legally sound, tailored to your state laws, and is designed to minimize taxes and maximize protection.

Don't wait for "someday" to complete estate planning. Start now. It is your responsibility to give your loved ones one less thing to worry about when it matters most.

CHAPTER 26

Generational Wealth: Keeping Your Family in the Game

There is a story about a man named Grandpa Kurt.

A Navy vet with a quiet spirit and a hustle that never quit. He worked two jobs and bought a modest duplex in the '70s.

Paid it off in 15 years and then decided to buy another one.

He never talked about money though, just about "leaving something behind."

By the time he passed, he had six rental properties, a pension, two paid-off cars, and a safety deposit box full of war medals and paperwork nobody understood.

The family buried him on a Friday and by Monday, the questions started flying.

"Who's supposed to take over the rentals?"
"What's this insurance policy for?"
"What does this trust mean?"
"Why is my name on the deed?"

And just like that... the foundation he'd built began to crack. This wasn't because he didn't care... this happened because no one knew the playbook.

Sadly, this isn't just a story. It describes a pattern that plays out in real life almost every day.

70% of families lose their wealth by the second generation. 90% lose it by the third.
This common outcome is not due to carelessness, it happens so often because the important information dies with the person who built the wealth.

Grandpa Kurt left money.
But not instructions.

Assets.
But no strategy.

He created generational opportunity.
But not generational readiness.

Then Came Nia

Kurt's 32 year old granddaughter. She works in marketing, has two kids, and a very curious mind.

After the dust settled, she started asking better questions. Started reading documents and found Grandpa Kurt's bank statements.

She sat down with a financial advisor, and what she uncovered was much more than just money. She discovered wealth potential.

She created a checklist, and over time she was able to:

- Reorganized the properties under an LLC
- Created a family trust
- Paid off "back taxes"
- Drafted her own will, and encouraged her siblings to do the same
- Started documenting every conversation, decision, and dollar in a binder labeled: "The James Legacy Playbook"(James being the family name).

What did Nia do differently?
For starters, she didn't treat wealth like a mystery, but like a system.

She made financial literacy a family language.
She opened a custodial account for her son and hosted "Family Finance Fridays" online with the rest of her family where she'd break down insurance, taxes, and estate planning.

She wasn't trying to be the smartest person in the room; she was trying to make sure her kids wouldn't be the most confused person at the reading of her will.

Nia is creating "Generational Wealth", not to be confused with an inheritance. She ensured that on top of the money, systems and knowledge were passed down. Her family understood the "why", which allowed them to move differently with the "what".

If you've gotten this far in the playbook, you're already building. But now it's time to ask yourself some very important questions.

Will your kids know how to use what you leave behind?

Will they understand why you made the moves you made?

Will they be good stewards... or just recipients?

The only thing separating generational wealth from generational regret is preparation.

If your story ended today, what would your family inherit?

A house and confusion? Or a blueprint and confidence?

Start now.

- Record your process
- Teach what you've learned
- Document the steps
- And make sure your playbook is bigger than you

Because true legacy doesn't end with your last dollar.
It starts with your first conversation.

CHAPTER 27

Navigating Taxes: The Secrets of the Wealthy

We've mentioned this a few times now, but it's very important to understand that tax education is one component on your wealth journey designed to give you a sharper lens on how taxes work. As you read through and complete this chapter, consider your own personal finances. Don't hesitate to consult a licensed tax advisor when making personal or business-related tax decisions. With that out the way, let's peel back the secrets of the wealthy.

Here's what most people do:
-Work a job
  -Get a paycheck
    -Pay taxes before they ever touch their money
      -Cross their fingers for a refund in April
        -Call it a day

But the wealthy are playing a completely different game. They understand that taxes can be your biggest expense in life. Meaning, if you don't know how to manage them, they'll eat your income, your growth, and your legacy alive. Sounds scary, but the wealthy don't fear taxes. They strategize around them. Asking questions like "how can I convert income into assets?" Or "How can I legally lower my taxable income?"

They aren't cheating the system, they understand it.

If the idea of taxes ever confused you, then this chapter is for you. Next, we are going to get into the moves, tools, and strategies that keep more money in your pocket instead of giving it all to Uncle Sam.

1. Know Your Bracket and Use It

Did you know that the U.S. has a progressive tax system? This means your income is taxed in tiers, and not all at once. For example, if you are in the 24% bracket, not all your income is taxed at 24%. Only the income in that specific range is.

Understanding this method of being taxed can help you time your income in lower earning years or plan your retirement withdrawals wisely. It also gives you an idea of how you need to consider reducing your taxable income.

2. Use Tax-Advantaged Accounts

We talked about most of these already, but here is a refresher. These accounts can help you legally pay less in taxes today or tomorrow.

- 401(k) / 403(b) - traditional reduces current taxable income; Roth gives tax-free growth
- IRA / Roth IRA - same idea; income limits apply
- HSA (Health Savings Account) - triple tax advantage (deductible in, grows tax-free, and tax-free withdrawals for health)
- 529 Plans - tax-advantaged college, trade license, and other post grade school opportunity savings

These accounts are Legal shelters that the government encourages you to use. Choose the one that makes the most sense for you.

3. Business Owners and Entrepreneurs

This next section is for my business owners. Your business unlocks a new tax world where deductions are your best friend.

- Internet, phone, and a portion of your home office
- Software and supplies
- Travel, meals (with limits), and education
- Mileage and transportation
- Even retirement contributions via SEP IRA or Solo 401(k)

When done right, your business becomes your greatest tax strategy.

**Pro tip: Keep receipts and a mileage log of all business expenses. The IRS doesn't play when it comes to taxes, so if you are ever audited, a paper trail will serve as good evidence.*

4. Capital Gains vs. Ordinary Income

When it comes to getting taxed, the IRS will primarily hit you in one of two ways. Capital gains or ordinary income. Ordinary income is anything that falls under wages, tips, or your salary. You will get taxed at your income bracket for ordinary income.

Then there's capital gains tax. This tax is applied to the realized profit that is made when an asset is sold.

Capital gains can be broken down further into short-term capital gains and long-term capital gains. Short-term is any asset that is bought and sold within a 12 month period.

The profit on these will be taxed at your taxable income level. Long-term capital gains are profits from an asset that is held longer than 12 months. These gains have the benefit of being taxed at a lower tax bracket (0%, 15%, or 20%) depending on your taxable income.

5. Real Estate

Real estate offers a unique combo of cash flow + appreciation + tax benefits:

- Depreciation - paper loss that reduces taxable income
- Mortgage interest deduction
- 1031 Exchanges – defer taxes by reinvesting into new property
- Cost segregation – accelerate depreciation to reduce taxes now

And if you become a real estate professional by IRS standards, you unlock even more aggressive tax deductions.

6. Charitable Giving Lowers Taxes

Want to give back and get a break?

- Donate to qualified nonprofits
- Use Donor-Advised Funds (DAFs) for long-term giving
- Donate appreciated assets (like stock) instead of cash to avoid capital gains

Being generous can lower your taxable income and raise your legacy impact.

A good tax professional can see things you might miss. They can suggest entity structures, calculate depreciation timelines, and create personalized year-round tax plans. Hiring one is an investment that will allow you to keep more of what you earned each year.

This chapter isn't meant to make you a tax expert, but it is meant to help you realize that taxes are not an "April problem". Learn to play the game year-round.

CHAPTER 28

Cyber & Identity Security: Protect Your Digital Wealth From Scams

Imagine waking up one day and your bank account is frozen, credit cards are completely maxed out, a loan you never applied for just hit your credit report, and on top of all that, someone filed your taxes and claimed your tax refund.

You didn't lose your money on a bad investment, or splurge on something you couldn't afford.

You got played by a scammer.

In the digital age, your money is only as safe as your data. You can have a six-figure salary, a perfect credit score, and a solid portfolio. That can all go out the window if a cybercriminal gets your information. With the right details, they can flip your life upside down. It's called social engineering, and it's a real threat.

Social engineers don't hack code. they hack you. They pull at your human emotions, like urgency and trust. Here's how it usually plays out:

- A "bank rep" calls, claiming there's fraud on your account and requests more info
- A text from "UPS" says your package couldn't be delivered
- A popup warns you your device is infected and needs immediate cleaning

And with artificial intelligence on the rise, scammers are starting to look more legit than ever.

We bring this chapter as awareness to help you see what is at risk if you aren't vigilant online.

- Your savings
- Your retirement accounts
- Your credit score
- Your tax refunds
- Your identity
- Your entire financial reputation

Once a scammer gets your personal info (SSN, DOB, address, passwords), they can:

- Open credit cards in your name
- Drain bank or investment accounts
- File false tax returns
- Lock you out of your own digital life

Defending against these types of attacks should become part of your wealth tool box. Let's go over what you can implement today to protect yourself.

Use Strong, Unique Passwords

No more "Password123" or using the same one everywhere. Use a password manager to create and store complex passwords for every account.

Enable Two-Factor Authentication (2FA)

If someone guesses your password, this adds another layer. Use it for banking, email, social media or anywhere that matters.

Freeze Your Credit
Yes, you can actually do this, and it's free. This can stop scammers from opening new accounts in your name. You can just unfreeze your credit when you need to. Go to Equifax, Experian, and TransUnion to do it in under 30 minutes.

Don't Click Random Links
Scammers love emails and texts with "click here to verify" messages. Don't. If in doubt, go directly to the website or call the institution.

Monitor Your Accounts Weekly
Check your bank and credit accounts like you check social media. Catch fraud fast and act immediately.

Watch for Over-Sharing
Your social media says more than you think. Scammers use your birthday posts, job titles, even photos of your mail or keys to piece together your identity.

File Taxes Early
File early to avoid getting scammed out of your refund.

And here are some next level moves to add an extra layer of cyber protection:

- Sign up for identity theft protection with monitoring services (some banks offer this for free)
- Set up alerts for transactions over a certain amount
- Use trusted, encrypted apps for sensitive documents or communications
- Learn how to spot phishing emails (check the sender, spelling, and links)

You've come so far and there's no way you tracked every dollar, optimized every move, played the long gam, just to let a scammer walk off with your progress.

In today's world, cyber vigilance = wealth protection.

It's non-negotiable.

So stay alert and ask questions. Never trust and always verify. You worked to build your freedom, now guard it with the same tenacity that got you here.

CYBER THREAT DEFENSE CHECKLIST

Scammers use social engineering to deceive and steal. Here's how to fortify your defenses.

Strong Passwords
Use unique passwords for each account

Two-Factor Authentication
Add an extra step to your logins

Credit Freeze
Prevent scammers opening accounts in your name

Monitor Accounts
Review bank and credit accounts weekly

Don't Click Links
Beware emails or texts urging you to click

Guard Your Info
Limit sharing sensitive data-especially on social media

TYPES OF SOCIAL ENGINEERING ATTACKS

PHISHING

Fake emails asking for information or pushing links

SMISHING

Text messages in the same style

VISHING

Calls pretending to be banks, agencies, or compnies

BAITING

Too-good-to-be-true offers or malware on USB drives

CONGRATULATIONS

If you're reading this, then take a second to really acknowledge something important:

You showed up and you stayed with it!

You made the time to learn, reflect, and strategize for your financial future. That matters.

In a world full of distractions and shortcuts, you decided to do the work. And that work has equipped you with the foundation, awareness, and tools to move differently from this point forward.

You don't need to remember every single detail, but you do need to remember this:
This book is your playbook, not a one-time read.

Come back to it when you're stuck.
Reread a play when your season changes.
Flip through the pages when you need clarity, courage, or a course correction.

These plays don't expire, and neither does your ability to win.

But wait! the game's not over just yet... Because we've got one more section. A bonus quarter.

Welcome to the **Bonus Play: Overtime**, where we focus on the intangible assets that take your financial life from good to great.

BONUS PLAY

OVERTIME

UPSKILLING

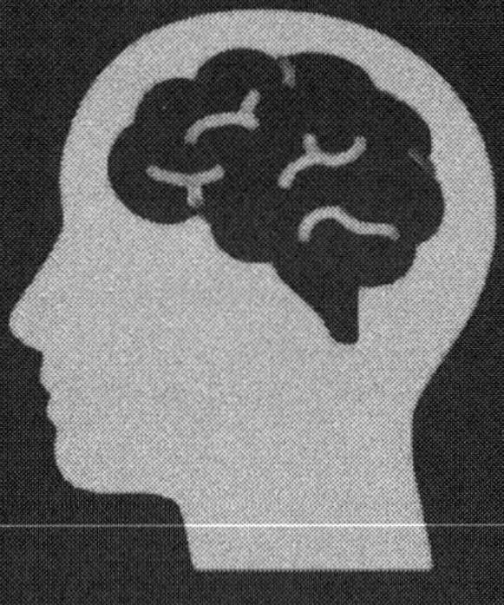

MENTAL WEALTH

GIVING BACK

FREEDOM

CHAPTER 29

Upskilling:
The Best ROI Is You

There's one investment you'll never lose money on.

No market crash can touch it.
No recession can reduce it.
No scammer can steal it.

It's you.

Your skills, your ability to gain knowledge, and your growth. We spend so much time thinking about where to put our money... but rarely stop to ask:

What if I became the most valuable asset in my entire portfolio?

Look behind almost every major financial breakthrough and you'll find one thing:
Someone learned something new. Maybe it was a new skill, or a new way of thinking. Regardless, the biggest shifts in wealth came from them leveling up before cashing in.

With your new wealthy mindset, you have to do more than just invest in the stock market or real estate. Start thinking about obtaining certifications, establishing a mentor, and gaining soft and hard skills. Your earning potential = your commitment to learning.

Not sure where to start? Ask yourself:

- What do people already come to me for help with?
- What do I love doing that I could monetize with better tools or training?
- What skill, if I mastered it, would make the next 5 years of my life easier?

Now pick a lane and get moving. Here are some high-ROI areas to explore:

- Tech & Digital
    - Ex. Data analysis, AI creation, cybersecurity
    - Why? High demand, remote-friendly
- Communication
    - Ex. Public speaking, negotiation, copywriting
    - Why? Influence = income
- Financial Literacy
    - Ex. Tax planning, investing, budgeting tools
    - Why? Protects and grows money
- Entrepreneurship
    - Ex. Branding, marketing offer creation
    - Why? Unlock multiple income streams
- Certification
    - Ex. Project management, trades, real estate
    - Why? Opens doors to new industries
- Degrees
    - Ex. Associates, Bachelors, Masters, PHD
    - Why? Networking and career opportunities

You made a plan for your money, and now you need to make a plan for yourself. Some of these might take time, but all can be worth it if you handle it right.

STEP 1: Choose one skill or area to master this year
STEP 2: Find 3 - 5 learning tools (courses, books, YouTube, podcasts)
STEP 3: Commit to 30 minutes per day
STEP 4: Track progress monthly
STEP 5: Apply what you learn in real time

Between YouTube University, LinkedIn Learning, Coursera, and free certifications, there is really no excuse for not upskilling. There is a path for every budget.

You can use upskilling to:

- Get a raise
- Land a better job
- Start a side hustle
- Negotiate smarter
- Avoid costly mistakes
- Lead a team
- Build something of your own

One skill can flip your trajectory, and one insight can shave years off your learning curve.

Your money works best when you know what to do with it. Your time pays back when you know how to use it. Your confidence grows when you keep promises to yourself. So don't just invest in stocks, and don't just buy courses just to let them collect digital dust.

Become the kind of person who turns knowledge into action. Become the most prepared person in the room. The one who never stops learning.

CHAPTER 30

Mental Wealth:
Health, Mindset, and Boundaries

You did the work! You fixed the mindset and made the sacrifices. You followed the six plays, and now you're winning. There's room for you to finally breathe easier and watch your money stretch and grow.

But with new levels come new... expectations.
The calls and subtle requests start pouring in. Someone asking for a "little help," telling you that "you got it right?" Suddenly your biggest challenge isn't how to build wealth, now it's how to protect your peace while keeping your heart intact.

Welcome to mental wealth where boundaries and balance are your friend.

Money is not just a physical item you grow and use, money is time spent, energy used, and decisions made. And if you having wealth means losing your sanity, can you really call that freedom?

Mental wealth means learning to give without draining, and being able to support without sacrificing your own stability.

And that means instilling boundaries and creating balance. Defining the limits of your financial help without feeling like you are pushing people away.

If you are the first in your family to do anything:

- First to invest
- First to graduate college
- First to make six figures
- First to break generational struggle

You might feel that tug, that invisible weight to bring everyone with you. But if you say "yes" to everyone, you could be saying "no" to future opportunities. There should be balance in giving back, a balance that keeps you sustainable without feeling "selfish."

"Smart giving" is giving with a strategy, because if we're being honest, we all want to give back. We want to be able to support our people and our community. But "random giving" without structure is how wealth disappears. It's how burnout begins and how resentment creeps in. In this chapter, we want to give some tips on being able to give back without burning out your mental.

1. Set a Generosity Budget

Pick a percentage (5%, 10%) of your income and decide how it's split:

- Family
- Community
- Causes you care about
- Emergency "I got you" fund

Once the budget's tapped, that's it for the month. No guilt. No overdrawn feelings.

2. Give Without Giving Money
Money is not your only asset. Besides giving your money, you can give:

- Time - Volunteer or mentor someone
- Knowledge - Teach others what you've learned
- Access - Introduce people to tools, platforms, or networks
- Encouragement - Share your story, not just your wallet

This is the quote *"Give a man a fish, and you feed him for a day. Teach a man to fish, and you feed him for a lifetime,"* put into motion.

3. Say "No" Without Burning Bridges
You can create redirection by saying things like:

- "That doesn't fit my financial plan right now."
- "Let's brainstorm together, I can help with ideas."
- "I'm building something for long-term impact, and I need to stay focused."

This doesn't make you heartless or cold. You are clearly stating what you can and cannot do. The people that care about you should understand.

4. Build Your Giving Vehicle
Once your income grows, formalize your generosity:

- Start a giving account
- Create a family support system with rules
- Support others through education, not just emergency cash apps

When you feel torn between giving and guarding, you can ask yourself these questions:

- **Am I helping or rescuing?**
- **Is this generosity or guilt?**
- **If I keep giving like this, what does my future look like?**
- **Is this level of help sustainable?**

Those answers should tell you everything you need to know.

You are the asset now and you are building a lasting legacy. One where mental boundaries are just as important as having a financial plan. Protect your peace, focus, and capacity. Give back when you can, but do not collapse from the weight of wanting to carry everyone on your back.

CHAPTER 31

Freedom: Defining Wealth on Your Own Terms

Pause for a moment and soak in this feeling of progress, because you made it.

You didn't get here by accident or blind luck, but by deciding that the next chapter of your life needed a different kind of blueprint. You've unlearned bad habits while challenging generational patterns. Building your foundation rooted in intention, clarity, and vision.

Now it's time to talk about freedom!

Most people think freedom means never working again or driving a certain car. But real freedom isn't about money, it's about options.

Freedom is you having the ability to wake up and live life on your terms without fear and pressure. Freedom is knowing your bills are paid before the 1st hits. It's watching your investments grow while you're asleep or walking into a store and not checking your account before you swipe. Freedom is not being owned by your job, your debt, or your guilt.

It's having options, and the power to say yes or no without flinching. But most importantly, freedom is defined by you. You decide what that looks like in your life. Not social media, society, your family, not even this book.

Just You.

So let's stop here for a sec and ask ourselves...

"What does freedom look like to me?"

Is it:

- Working part-time and still living well?
- Retiring your mom?
- Owning your schedule?
- Being debt-free?
- Creating a business you believe in?
- Traveling with no time limit?
- Having quiet mornings and full savings?

Write it down and name it. Because freedom undefined is freedom delayed.

You didn't just read a book.
You rebuilt the way you see money.
The way you see yourself.
The way you see your future.

You:

- Challenged old beliefs
- Faced your numbers
- Asked hard questions
- Laid a new foundation
- Built systems, not just goals
- Learned the language of wealth

Before we part ways, let us say this:

We see you. We honor you. We believe in the version of you that's still becoming.

This isn't the end of the playbook...
It's just the start of your new game.

Don't wait for permission.
Don't wait until your net worth hits a magic number.
Don't wait until you feel "ready."

GET OFF THE SIDELINES TODAY.

You have tools, momentum, and knowledge.

True freedom is when your money reflects your values and your time reflects your priorities,

So go define your version of wealth.
Define your version of impact.
And define your version of freedom.

THANK YOU FOR READING

To every reader who made it to this point, we thank you.

Thank you for trusting this book to guide your journey.
Thank you for showing up for your future.
Thank you for turning every page with purpose.

This was more than just you finishing a book. This was a commitment to yourself, your growth, and your legacy.

We hope these plays challenged you, encouraged you, and reminded you that wealth and financial freedom are both possible.

Wherever you are in your journey, remember that this playbook is always in your hands. You can run it back again and again if you need to.

Here's to building wealth and accomplishing freedom on your terms!

With gratitude,
The Investors Playbook Team

GLOSSARY

401(k) – A tax-advantaged retirement plan offered by employers, often with matching contributions.

403(b) – A retirement plan for employees of nonprofits and public schools, similar to a 401(k).

APR (Annual Percentage Rate) – The yearly interest charged on loans or earned on investments.

Asset – Anything of value owned, including cash, property, stocks, or businesses.

Automation – Setting up financial systems to run on autopilot, like auto-saving or recurring investing.

Budget – A financial plan for managing income and expenses over a set period.

Business Credit – Credit tied to a business entity rather than an individual.

Capital Appreciation – The increase in the value of an asset or investment over time.

Cash Flow – The movement of money in and out of your finances, including income and expenses.

Compound Effect – The snowballing impact of small, consistent actions over time.

Credit Bureau – Agencies (Equifax, Experian, TransUnion) that collect and report consumer credit data.

Credit Report – A detailed summary of your credit history used to determine creditworthiness.

Credit Score – A numerical representation of your credit risk based on your credit history.

Cybersecurity – The practice of protecting financial data and personal information online.

Debt Consolidation – Combining multiple debts into one with a lower interest rate or better terms.

Debt Snowball – A payoff strategy that focuses on clearing smaller debts first to build momentum.

Depreciation – The decrease in an asset's value over time, often used for tax purposes.

Diversification – Investing in different asset types to reduce risk.

Dividend – A portion of a company's profits paid to shareholders.

Emergency Fund – Savings set aside for unexpected expenses or financial crises.

Estate Planning – The process of preparing legal documents to manage your assets after death.

ETF (Exchange-Traded Fund) – A type of investment fund that's traded like a stock.

Fixed Expenses – Recurring costs that stay the same each month, such as rent or insurance.

Freedom – The ability to live life on your own terms without financial pressure.

Generational Wealth – Assets and knowledge passed down from one generation to the next.

Good Debt – Borrowed money used for productive purposes, like investing or education.

High-Interest Debt – Debt with a high APR, such as credit card balances.

Income Split – Dividing your paycheck automatically between checking, savings, and investing.

Inflation – The rise in prices over time, which erodes purchasing power.

Insurance – Financial protection against risk, including life, health, and property.

Interest – The cost of borrowing money or the return on invested funds.

Investment – Putting money into assets like stocks, real estate, or businesses for future gain.

IRA (Individual Retirement Account) – A tax-advantaged account for retirement savings.

Legacy – What you leave behind financially, emotionally, or generationally.

Leverage – Using borrowed money or assets to grow wealth or increase returns.

Liability – A financial obligation or debt.

Liquidity – How quickly an asset can be converted to cash.

Mental Wealth – The peace of mind and clarity that comes from financial stability and boundaries.

Mortgage – A loan used to buy real estate, paid back with interest over time.

Mutual Fund – A professionally managed collection of stocks, bonds, or other securities.

Net Worth – The difference between your total assets and total liabilities.

Opportunity Cost – What you give up when you choose one financial decision over another.

Overtime Play – The bonus section of your wealth journey focused on purpose, giving, and personal growth.

Passive Income – Money earned without active effort, such as rent or dividends.

Phishing – A form of cyber-attack where scammers trick individuals into giving up sensitive info.

Real Estate – Property or land used as an investment to build wealth through appreciation or income.

REIT (Real Estate Investment Trust) – A company that owns or finances income-producing real estate.

Return on Investment (ROI) – A measure of the gain or loss on an investment relative to its cost.

Rollover IRA – An IRA created by transferring funds from another retirement plan, like a 401(k).

Roth IRA – A retirement account funded with after-tax dollars; withdrawals are tax-free in retirement.

Savings Rate – The portion of income set aside for future use or emergencies.

Self-Directed IRA – A retirement account that allows investing in alternative assets like real estate.

SEP IRA – A retirement plan for self-employed individuals and small business owners.

Side Hustle – A secondary source of income outside your main job.

Term Life Insurance – A policy that provides coverage for a fixed number of years.

Trust – A legal entity that holds and manages assets on behalf of a beneficiary.

Upskilling – Learning new or enhanced skills to increase your earning potential.

Variable Expenses – Costs that change month to month, like groceries or gas.

Wealth – The accumulation of valuable resources and financial assets.

Whole Life Insurance – A permanent life insurance policy that includes a cash value component.

Will – A legal document stating how your assets should be distributed after your death.

INVESTOR'S PLAYBOOK RESOURCES

Made in the USA
Columbia, SC
17 August 2025

e1260500-a7e6-4c1d-8225-f5139362d8c8R01